PATCHES

PATCHES

BOOK 3

Our Lives, In The Hand Of The Master,
Come Together Like A Patchwork Quilt:
Beautifully Designed, Colorful, And Useful.

DIANA WARNER-ADAMS

XULON PRESS

Xulon Press
2301 Lucien Way #415
Maitland, FL 32751
407.339.4217
www.xulonpress.com

Paperback ISBN-13: 978-1-66286-316-5
Ebook ISBN-13: 978-1-66286-317-2

Dedication

P *atches* is dedicated to my two children, Michael and Diana. Their growing up years were the best part of my life. Their antics, dedication to learning, shared experiences, choosing of their mates and the births of their children gave meaning to my life. I will forever be grateful to God for giving them to me.

Children are indeed a gift from the Lord.

Introduction

RAINY SEASONS IN OUR LIVES

"He causes his sun to rise on the evil and the good, and sends rain on the righteous and the unrighteous." Matthew 5:45 (NIV)

R *ain, rain, go away; come again another day.*
Rainy seasons. They come and go. So do the rainy seasons in our lives.

In visiting with a friend by phone recently, she commiserated with me over the rainy season that had come into her life.

Her spouse of many years had passed away in the spring, just two days short of his 90th birthday. Now Jeanie was having to go it alone.

This was a new journey Jeanie was on and she was adapting as best she could. Through depending on her two sons who stopped in daily, connecting with a cousin for travel, and joining a book club, she was finding the days manageable and, to a degree, pleasurable.

I too had travelled the same road my friend was now traveling.

And, like Jeanie, I too made the best of my days. Some days were lonely but some days were filled with joy and satisfaction. Family, of course, made a difference, as did spending time with friends and being involved with my church.

Scripture gives sound advice on living life to the fullest. Jesus himself said that we are not to give ourselves over to anxiety but we are rather to put God first in our lives and everything would fall into place.

While this may seem simplistic, I have found this really works.

Widowed for over ten years and, in the beginning, struggling to maintain a balance in my life, I finally learned that excessive worrying wasn't profitable for my physical, mental or spiritual health.

Starting anew, I began the day on a positive note. I studied and applied Scripture to my circumstances. Little by little, trust came and God began to move in surprising ways.

In time, through the Social media, I met my husband Jay.

Transplanted and now living in Georgia, I find my whole life has done a complete 180.

Serving in ministry at a particular Baptist church and interfacing with the church community as a whole has brought much satisfaction to my life. Working alongside my husband in a supportive role, I sense a new commitment to our Lord.

Whoever could have known?

At the time of Russ'[1] demise, I claimed a familiar Scripture as a personal promise: *"For I know the thoughts that I think toward you, says the LORD, thoughts of peace and not of evil, to give you a future and a hope."* (Jeremiah 29:11, NKJV)

While there were times I wavered and lacked trust, God remained faithful.

In His time and in His way, he brought J. L. and me together for his purposes.

And each time there's an opportunity, I tell our story on the off chance it may encourage someone out there who is struggling as I once was.

My story, I believe, may give them that spark of hope they're looking for.

Don't give up, I tell them. Our God is the God of the impossible. He sees. He knows. He loves. He cares.

Believe and receive all that He has for you. In time your Rainy Season, like mine, will give way to a silver lining.

Table of Contents

Chapter 1

Paul and Angie

Blessed are those who mourn, for they will be comforted. Matthew 5:4 (NIV)

Paul and Angie sat across from Jay and me in a corner booth at a popular restaurant chain in Milledgeville, Georgia. The year was 2016. It was December, just before Christmas. Jay had called Paul and suggested the four of us get together so the two men could introduce their wives to each other.

We had all lost our mates and, providentially, met and married new mates in 2012.

After a pleasant meal and light conversation, Jay then encouraged Paul and Angie to share the circumstances under which they met.

"It was at a grief support class I started at our church after my wife died," Paul offered. "I wasn't looking to meet anyone," he explained, almost apologetically, "I just wanted to give others a chance to share what they might be going through."

Angie—a bright, bubbly, attractively dressed lady in her late sixties or early seventies—explained why she had gone to that first meeting.

"I wasn't looking to meet anyone," she, like Paul, assured us, "I wasn't intending to remarry. I guess I just wondered what they do at a grief class."

She, too, sounded a little apologetic.

Jay and Paul had been friends for some time. They were both ministers of the Gospel. Jay was presently doing interim work at a church near our home in Claxton, Georgia, and Paul was serving in a church in Milledgeville whose congregation had dwindled over time.

Both Jay and I listened attentively as the couple, clearly enamored with each other, shared with us how they had decided to date and ultimately to marry.

The interesting part for us was that Paul had called Jay in late November, 2012, to tell him he met someone and they were planning to marry on December 12. *"Will you marry us?"* Paul asked sprightly.

Jay, excited for Paul, gave him time to share his good news. Then he countered with: *"Paul, I'd love to marry you and Angie but I, too, have met someone and we plan to marry on December 9 in Pennsylvania! I won't be able to marry you because we'll be on our honeymoon!"*

The men, of course, just hooted and began hi-five-ing each other over the phone.

I couldn't hear what Paul was saying, nor, I imagine, could Angie hear what Jay was saying, but we could envision how special the news was to each of them.

As circumstances would have it, we hadn't gotten together before we met at the restaurant that evening, but each time we have since then, I've been reminded of what God said in His Word: *"I will turn your mourning into dancing" (Psa. 30:11).*

While many of us feel our life is over when we lose our mates—whether through death or divorce—often it's just an open door to something God turns into a new life and new learning experience for us.

Chapter 2

A Widow's Challenge

You will go out in joy and be led forth in peace;
the mountains and hills will burst into song
before you, and all the trees of the field will
clap their hands. Isaiah 55:12 (NIV)

I t was 3 a.m. The neighborhood was asleep and I was enjoying tea and crackers in my comfy living room.

My Ryrie Study Bible was opened on my lap to Isaiah. Alternatively, I read and pondered, first, the passage in Isaiah 54:5, *"For your Maker is your husband—the LORD Almighty is his name—the Holy One of Israel is your Redeemer; he is called the God of all the earth" (NIV).* Then I turned to a familiar passage in the book of Ruth.

Ruth, you'll remember, was the young widow from Moab who valiantly embraced the God of her mother-in-law, Naomi, and, trusted Him to take care of them both.

Together, Naomi and Ruth, tired and hungry, travelled to Bethlehem, Ruth pledging to take care of the older woman until death parted them.

"Don't urge me to leave you or to turn back from you," Ruth begged Naomi when encouraged to go back to her people. *"Where you go I will go, and where you stay I will stay. Your people will be my people and your God my God. Where you die I will die, and there I will be buried" (Ruth 1:16-17).*

As students of the Scriptures, we know how the story ended: Both Ruth and Naomi were taken care of through Boaz, the rich landowner who embraced his responsibility as *kinsman-re-deemer* to Naomi.[2]

It would be through Ruth and Boaz' union that the future king of Israel, David, would be born. And, more importantly, it was through David's line that our Savior, the Lord Jesus Christ, would to be manifested to all Israel as well as, ultimately, to the rest of the world.

One of the decisions many of us have to make when we lose our mates is: *Should I sell my home or should I stay where I am and try to maintain it on my own?*

Sometimes the decision hinges on financial obligations, or it may depend on physical or emotional needs.

Often there may be other decisions to consider as well, such as moving closer to a son or daughter for emotional or phys-ical support. Or wanting to free oneself up from responsibility. Or trying to look too far into the future, not realizing that God alone determines our future, both from the standpoint of health as well as our ability to manage our own affairs.

Age counts, too. Naturally, an older person will have con-cerns that will differ from a younger person's who is still quite capable of being independent.

Sometimes challenges are compounded by family members' needs or wishes.

Because, originally, I'm from eastern Canada and owned, at that time, a summer home there, I was torn between living there and staying in Pennsylvania. But I had my daughter, Diana, and her family to think of. If I left her, would she think I was deserting her?

As it turned out, I eventually sold my home in Canada. But by this time, Diana had become so involved with her preteens' school, sports and church activities that she had little time to spend with me. She and Dave both assured me, of course, that I was always welcome to visit them. And this I did, often.

Diana's circumstances, of course, would change in a few years time but, for then, I had to work around her schedule, planning my visits to coincide with her family's time.

I do need to add here, though, that had Diana not made herself available to me on countless occasions, I would not have been able to travel as I did. Trips back and forth to the airport fighting heavy traffic, either to drop me off or to pick me up, would have kept me from spending time in Nova Scotia.

When it finally became apparent I needed to sell the house Russ and I had purchased there together just prior to his demise, Diana helped me by making phone calls from her end. This saved me a lot of expense and trouble and I will ever be grateful to her for that.

This also added to her responsibilities at a time when Dave was traveling and the children were dependent on her to meet their daily needs.

All this is to say that widowhood brings change. And while one person's circumstances differs from another's, there's still the need to take each day as it comes.

Having a positive attitude and waking each morning with the realization that Christ is *with* you and *in* you and has a wonderful plan for your life brings vitality to each new day as well.[3]

Finding your niche in service is important, too. After selling my primary home in Exeter Township, PA, I rather quickly joined in membership with a local group of believers in Myerstown, about 50 miles west of Reading. I purchased a home in a 55-plus community new to that area. This put me close to an independent Baptist church nearby. Soon after joining, I was asked to fill a moderator's vacancy in the ladies' Sunday school class. Through this, I made several close friends. These friends, along with my daughter and her family, were my life's source of ministry and heart's joy.

In time, four to six of us single ladies would meet at my home after church to have lunch together. And while most often I prepared the meal, others would contribute as well. One lady in particular brought a full-course meal on several occasions. This freed me up to put the finishing touches on the meal and get it on the table.

Two of the ladies enjoyed working on the puzzle set up in the heated sun porch while waiting for the meal. Then, afterward, we would visit in the living room. Here we'd enjoy a devotional and discussion time before they left for home.

God is good! All this is to say that those of us who have lost our life's mate may have to work a little harder at finding meaning for our lives. But by keeping our focus on the Lord and making each day count for him, we *can* live happy, productive lives.

Prayer: Dear Jesus, please help me, as a widow, to not dwell on what I have lost but rather to dwell on what, with your help, I will gain if I reach out to others.

Chapter 3

Financial Planning

Sow your seed in the morning, and at evening
let your hands not be idle, for you do not know
which will succeed, whether this or that, or
whether both will do equally well. Ecclesiastes
11:1 (NIV)

Twenty-seven years ago and nearing retirement, Russ suggested we contact a financial advisor.

At first, I was opposed to the idea. After all, we had taken
care of our own finances for years and we hadn't had a problem.
Even in the lean years, we had used wisdom and, with God's
help, were able to make ends meet.

Why on earth would he want to do this now? I wondered.

But it was a decision, I believe, he had already made. He
was just asking me to go along with it.

And so I did. And, to this day, I am glad I did.

At first when we visited Roy, I didn't listen attentively. I'd
never been a lover of figures and while I had, over the years,
taken my turn at writing checks and sharing financial decisions

made for the household and the children, each time we visited Roy, I picked up more and more.

And then, in 2002, when Russ was diagnosed with a terminal disease, I knew enough to recognize that I would need help with future responsibilities in this area.

And while my adult children have always been very helpful in answering any questions I might have about finances, they very graciously allowed me the option of doing whatever I felt was necessary in this area. After all, they had their own families to think about and they couldn't always be there for me.

After meeting with the owner of the financial firm alone that first time, I realized it would be difficult for me to communicate my needs with Roy. This led to my switching, with Roy's permission, to an individual who was an associate at the firm.

From the moment I met Doug, I knew we would be able to work together. For one thing, Doug's widowed mom was living with him and his family and his widowed mother-in-law was just a few blocks away.

Since I was newly widowed, there was an instant bond. I felt from the onset that I could trust Doug to advise me on future concerns I might have with regards to my finances.

Well, that was a number of years ago. Doug and I have had a couple of crisis moments when we didn't see eye to eye, but only once have I ever considered looking for another advisor. Doug's love for the Lord, as well as his compassion for me as someone living on her own, has meant more to me than he could ever imagine.

The point of all this is simply to say: There are many areas of responsibility a widow must take on. One is in the area of finances. If you do not have a close family member who can do this for you, consider seeking out a godly Christian firm who will share this responsibility with you.

An advisor who will pray with you before getting down to business is someone who will make himself accountable for the way he handles your investments.

In the end, this may make the difference between your being able to live well comfortably into old age and having to seek relief through some other source.

As it turned out, I was on my own for just over ten years. Then the Lord graciously brought Jay into my life, a semi-retired pastor who himself had been widowed, not once but twice.

And while it meant a move South, I have been blessed in so many ways in the nine years J.L. and I have been married. Incidentally, I still handle my own finances and, should the Lord take J.L. home before me, I have the ability and means to take care of myself in this area.

It's a comfortable feeling and one I would pray others who find themselves in this same situation might take to heart.

Prayer: Dear Jesus, You have promised to never leave us nor forsake us. Help us, each one, to trust and rely on your promises and on the people you bring into our lives to guide us. Amen.

Chapter 4

A Grief Class: Is It Right For You?

The Lord is near. Do not be anxious about anything, but in every situation, by prayer and petition, with thanksgiving, present your requests to God. And the peace of God, which transcends all understanding, will guard your hearts and your minds in Christ Jesus. Philippians 4:6-7 (NIV)

We finished up our ladies' Sunday school class with a brief discussion on *grief*. And because several in our group were widows, we compared notes on how important it is to have support while approaching or walking in widowhood.

How important is it, for instance, to attend a grief class? Personally speaking, I would say in retrospect, it's a good idea. Back then, I just wanted to *move on*. Others said this was their experience too. But *moving on* too quickly is not always a good idea, particularly if there are practical issues that need to be addressed.

While the Holy Spirit sends comfort through friends and family, availing oneself of a grief class will give a recently bereaved widow the opportunity to build an individual support system that is peculiar to her particular needs.

Many women, in the past, have depended on their husband for emotional, as well as, practical support. With that support no longer in place for them, they have to look to other sources for help. The woman who has made Christ the center of her life and is not a stranger to prayer or to Bible study will find her widow's walk more purposeful. But she will still need to face issues that are unique to her set of circumstances. A *good* grief class will address these issues and give her the tools and resources she will need to continue her earthly pilgrimage alone.

How does one find a grief class?

Many churches advertise the fact that they have one. If you are already attending church, your church may have a grief class already in place. If it's hard for you to take that first step, ask a friend to go with you. After the first or second session, you will feel more comfortable about going alone—or you may want to reach out to another recently widowed lady in your church to go with you.

What do they do in a grief class?

Here's where you need to investigate a little. Go on line and do a search, or pick up a brochure at the funeral home that conducted your husband's funeral, or ask someone who has already been through one.

The main thing is, do not let the fact that you have never been to one stop you from going. Incidentally, you will find many excuses or reasons why you shouldn't go. Don't give in to these excuses. If it's raining when you planned to attend your first grief class, remember it won't always be raining when you step outside.

Does a family member need you? Admittedly, that is a reason you need to consider. Family should come first. But if you get started and this happens more than once or twice, then ask that family member if they can get someone else to fill in for you. If they'll listen, tell them why you think attending the grief class is important to you.

Something to ask yourself if you decide to attend a grief class:

Why am I here? Am I hoping to meet someone to replace my recently departed loved one? Or am I looking for a friend who will help fill my lonely hours? Someone to share a meal with, go to a movie with, or help you with your errands and chores.

Some women may feel guilty if they get into another relationship too soon. Others are looking for someone they can bond with and ultimately marry. You should decide in your heart what's important to you. And of course, there's family to consider as well. They love you and are looking out for you. Try to include them in any decisions you may make for the future. In the long run, it will pay off and they will know you have their best interests at heart as well.

As with Paul and Angie, Paul's Grief Class brought them together. They have been married almost ten years now and to the naked eye, they certainly seem to have found much in each other to love and appreciate. Surely, it was a match made in heaven.

This leads me to my last thought: While losing our mate is not something most of us would choose, coming together in matrimony with another who has experienced a similar loss will provide that bonding and companionship we often look for, especially as we grow older.

Few of us want to spend long evenings alone in front of the television or stay away from special events when we could share the company of someone for whom we have a mutual attraction.

But there are risks involved in reaching out to someone you've met only recently, particularly if this someone sweeps you off your feet and presses you to make a commitment too quickly.

Conversely, there's the individual who leads you to believe he's looking to settle down for the duration but does not have marriage in mind. Here's where your good, sound relationship with the Lord is invaluable. If you've been faithful to read and to study and to meditate on his Word, then you be able to look for your answers here.

The Scripture says in Psa. 73:23-24, "Yet I am always with you; you hold me by my right hand. You *guide me with your counsel,* and afterward you will take me into glory."(*Emphasis, mine.*)

A good friend or friends with whom you can confide are priceless when you have a life-changing decision to make. We all have friends we feel we can trust, but it's best to stick to only one or two whose trustworthiness has been proven over time. My friend, Ruth,[4] for instance was my *someone* when I lived in Pennsylvania. Shortly after Jay had contacted me by phone,[5] I shared the essence of his calls with her. When Ruth learned Jay was a retired pastor and a widower who was looking for a "life's mate" to finish out his years with, she expressed her approval.

She also told me with a grin that she "felt quite sure" he would want to visit me soon. *And this he did! In less than two months after we met!*

Things progressed rather quickly after that and, on his third trip to Myerstown, PA, we were married.

Section II

An Answer to Prayer

Chapter 5

Jay

"Isaac brought her [Rebekah] into the tent of his mother Sarah, and he married Rebekah. So she became his wife, and he loved her; and Isaac was comforted after his mother's death."
Genesis 24:67 (NIV)

It was to be the second visit Jay would make to see me and I waited with anticipation at the Harrisburg International Airport in Pennsylvania for his plane to land and for him to come striding up the arrivals ramp.

The time frame was mid-to-late October. The ride over from Myerstown had been beautiful with the changing colors of fall painting the landscape. I hoped Jay would notice the vibrancy of the colors and perhaps, silently at least, compare them to the less vibrant colors he was used to in southeastern Georgia.

I don't recall what I was wearing that day, but I do know I chose something that would catch his eye. Jay was drawn to women who were attractively dressed. Not only had he told me that in several of our phone conversations, but I picked up on that myself the first time he came to meet me.

I didn't want to disappoint him. And I knew he wouldn't disappoint me either. He did cater to wearing jeans but they were a cut above the denims men wear to work. He liked the Saddlebred brand with the permanent crease in the pant leg. With his six-foot-one frame, they looked at home on him.

I was a bit early when I got to the airport, so I parked myself on a bench where I would have good visibility to watch him come up the ramp.

Within a few minutes, a pleasant woman, younger than I but not real young, joined me on my bench.

"*Hello*, she said." "*Hello*," I responded, courteously.

Then, warming to each other, we began to chat.

"Who are you waiting for?" I asked.

Talking to strangers has not been difficult for me since I gave my life to Jesus. Prior to that, I would shy away from conversations with people, even some I knew.

As she shared with me her reason for being at the airport at that time of day, I took note that she was attractively dressed in blue jeans, a short blouse, and a cute jacket over her petite frame.

She also had a small leather bag slung over her shoulder that matched her pricey-looking leather boots.

When Mavis[6] in turn asked me who I was there to meet, I told her. Now, *she* was the one who expressed curiosity. This led to my sharing with her how I met Jay.

But first I shared my experience on being a widow.

I also told Mavis how I had prayed every day to Jesus Christ, asking Him to bring a *good* Christian man into my life.

And I shared about the seemingly long wait and my reaching out online to make friends.[7]

Finally, I shared my connection with the man I was anxiously waiting to greet there that day, the man who, although I wouldn't know it then, would become my husband.

"Wow!" she exclaimed. "That's really something!"

"Yes, it is," I said, nodding my head in agreement.

"I wonder how many women this could this happen to in one lifetime?"

"I don't really know," I responded, "But, honestly, I truly wanted to remarry but I wasn't meeting anyone. At least, no one who shared my love for Jesus Christ.

"There wasn't anyone in our church I felt I could bond with, and the one individual I met in Nova Scotia during the time I spent up there in the summer was of a different mindset.

"I think we both knew from the onset that marriage wouldn't work. He wisely shied away from making a commitment. Although I was somewhat disappointed at the time, I felt I learned something from the experience."

My new acquaintance gave me her full attention. "And what was that?" she asked, inquisitively.

"That we must keep alert to how Satan would deceive us in our relationships.

"Ronald,[8] for instance, was very controlling. After I returned home to Pennsylvania at summer's end, he kept me on the phone for hours every evening. He also kept me in turmoil over my relationship with Jesus Christ.

"He did this for several years.

"He claimed to be a Christian—he asked to be baptized in the Baptist Church in the small community in which he lived—and I was witness to that.

"And he took me to church every Sunday where we worshipped together with other believers.

"But he couldn't or wouldn't embrace biblical theology; i.e., that the Lord God is one God in three Persons—Father, Son, and Holy Spirit.[9]

"This must have been very difficult for you," Mavis said, kindheartedly.

"Yes, it was—in part, because I have a strong belief in the work of the Holy Spirit in the life of a believer. The Bible actually reveals in Romans 8:26-27 that He "intercedes" in our prayers to God."

She nodded.

"There are many Scripture verses that affirm His work in every Christ-follower."

Her nod, I felt, gave me the go-ahead to share Christ with her.

"And while some misinterpret the work of the Spirit in an individual, Paul's letter to the church at Rome made it clear for me:

> *In the same way, the Spirit helps us in our weakness. We do not know what we ought to pray for, but the Spirit himself intercedes for us through wordless groans. And he who searches our hearts knows the mind of the Spirit, because the Spirit intercedes for God's people in accordance with the will of God. (Rom. 8:26-27, NIV. Emphasis, mine.)*

I could see by her attentiveness I had piqued Mavis' interest but, by now, Jay's plane evidently had landed as, one by one, people were coming up the ramp.

I recalled later that Mavis hadn't told me who she was waiting for. Perhaps I never gave her a chance. But suddenly, there was Jay, big as life, and grinning from ear to ear as he spotted me.

We embraced, briefly, both a little embarrassed as we hadn't embraced in public before. But soon we were on our way to Myerstown where we would share a meal at the popular Country Fare restaurant.

This particular visit, then, would last about five days. At the end of the visit as Jay prepared to leave for Georgia, we both knew in our hearts that our relationship would grow if given a chance.

Up to this time, Jay hadn't shared with his four children how serious he was about taking another mate. He didn't want to upset them if nothing came of it.

He had, however, on his return to his hometown area two-to-three years earlier, purchased a home that would accommodate a woman. One he hoped she would learn to love. This, he said later, quite possibly made them a little curious, but nothing was said to him at the time.

The crux of it was, we wanted to be together. We made our plans for a December wedding. So when Jay left on his return flight to Georgia, I sat by his side. I think we were both excited when the plane touched down in Savannah, knowing that we would soon connect with his family.

Chapter 6

Meeting Jay's Family

*Wives, submit yourselves to your own hus-
bands as you do to the Lord. For the husband
is the head of the wife as Christ is the head of
the church, his body, of which he is the Savior.
Ephesians 5:22 (NIV) (Emphasis, mine.)*

Jay had arranged that we all meet at a particular restaurant in
Vidalia on Tuesday evening. In the meantime, his daughter
Susan had suggested Jay arrange for me to stay at the Smith
Inn in Claxton.

I soon learned that it was an older Victorian-type house
filled with beautiful antiques.

I loved it.

There were lovely plants on the covered front porch as we
drove up, along with rockers if a person cared to be outdoors.

And there was a beautiful flower garden in the backyard.
The proprietor, Rose Callaway, lived in a smaller home in the
back corner of the property and maintained the property herself.

"You're welcome to enjoy the garden," she said, with a flourish, when Jay introduced me to her and settled me in from our flight.

Cold drinks we soon discovered were available in a commercial machine in the foyer and hot drinks, too, if one cared to prepare them. Freshly baked cookies, Rose said, were available in late afternoon for nibblers or any young children that would be house guests.

Everything appeared to be in place to make the visitor feel at home.

It was a delightful setting and I felt like a spoiled kitten when later I showered and got ready for dinner.

That evening, crawling into the beautifully made bed covered with pillows and linens fit for a princess, I had to pinch myself to see if what I was experiencing was real.

I was afraid I might wake up and, like Cinderella of Fairy Tale fame, find my prince and my pumpkin coach had disappeared with a *poof* as I slumbered peacefully.

But it was real and it was so very special.

Since meals were not served at the Inn, Jay picked me up at 9 each morning for breakfast. Then he shared with me his plans for our day. These, by the way, included many practical things most married couples do as they share their lives together: grocery shopping, errands, church, a day at the beach, and so on.

Jay, obviously, had thought of everything. He didn't want to buy a pig in a poke, so to speak, but rather try to learn as much as he could about his future wife before he committed himself to a permanent relationship.

I appreciated his practicality.

And I was alert to the way he communicated with his girls. His one son, Lewey, seemed to be happy for his dad. I felt his acceptance right away. It meant, and still means, a great deal to me.

The three girls, Nora, Susan, and Rebekah, I soon learned, all had different personalities and temperaments. They all, though, loved their dad dearly and it was obvious from that first meeting in the Vidalia restaurant, that they had his happiness at heart.

I knew from the onset that I would never replace their mother, Jane, nor did I intend to try. Mothers are special people. We have only one. And while our dads might remarry,[10] we need to accept the fact that we will never have the same relationship with that person that once we had with our birth mother.

Acceptance, though, warms the heart. And where everyone is committed to that, it will keep the family from drifting apart.

The spouses have a lot to do with it, too. I warmed to Lewey's wife, Joy, right away. She is a precious individual who reaches out to all whom the Lord brings into their lives. I feel blessed to be one of them.

Nora, Jay's oldest daughter, and her son, Joshua, made me feel welcome from the get-go. Reaching out in love, they drew me into their circle immediately, physically throwing their arms around me and making me feel at home.

Susan, Jay's second daughter, is by nature a little more reticent. She had her concerns which she voiced to her dad on several occasions, but she has shown me acceptance in that she's always ready to help out when and where she can.

Perhaps her personality is a little more like mine than the others. She's gracious but holds back a little until she's satisfied the person is genuine.

I can relate to that and appreciate Susan for that aspect of her personality.

Rebekah and Charles live near Vidalia. We saw little of them on my first visit to Jay's home because of their work schedules and their family routines. "Rebekah," Jay shared with me, "is the youngest and the most independent. She makes her own decisions and she and Charles live their own lives. She was only seventeen when Jane and I left for Seminary, and she and Charles married early."

I could tell by Jay's facial expression and his demeanor as he shared with me about each one that he was a loving and a caring dad. I was glad to see this as I knew he would be loving and accepting of my two children and my six grandchildren as well.

This meant, if we married, he would not prevent me from seeing them when I wanted to.

Earm and Greg, Nora and Susan's husbands, have shown me respect (as they all have, including the grandchildren) from Day One. Later, they would go on to meet needs when they were there and to include me as family—almost as if I'd always been there.

My visit to Claxton went all too quickly and soon I was boarding my plane for Philadelphia.

One highlight of the visit was our decision, mine and Jay's, to set the date for our wedding. Jay had taken me to the Mall one day and had me pick out an engagement ring. I chose a lovely solitaire diamond set in white gold.

Together, we picked out our wedding rings. Since mine had to be cut to size, Jay suggested he keep them there and he would bring them with him when he came up for our December wedding.

I agreed.

After that, we talked on the phone every evening and some-times in the early morning. We missed each other very much. And as every woman knows, this was a good sign for it meant we were longing for that day when we would be man and wife.

CRCRCRCRCRCR

I continued my nightly habit of going before the Lord in the wee hours of the morning. I knew in my heart, had it not been for Jesus Christ, my prayers for a mate at this stage in my life would never have been answered.

Surely, Jay must have felt the same way. Truly, we both had much to be thankful for.

We remain thankful to this day and often tell each other so and, in prayer, we praise God for his faithfulness.

Here I would be remiss if I did not mention we had the blessing of my daughter Diana, her husband, Dave, and their three children.

In that regard, I had arranged through the week for Diana and Dave, Davey, Casey and Tommy to come for dinner before Jay's second visit had ended. This would give them an opportu-nity to get acquainted with Jay (J. L.). Additionally, they would be able to ask him any questions that, perhaps, would concern all of us should we decide to marry.

The dinner went well. Diana and Dave seemed to be com-fortable with Jay's appearance, mannerisms, and interests. Jay appeared comfortable, too. He'd been in ministry for a goodly portion of his latter years and was used to meeting and greeting people, so there was really no reason for him not to be.

Chapter 7

The Wedding

Kathy, my dear friend who lived just a few doors down from me, was invaluable to me in the planning and execution of our wedding. She was active in the community—certainly moreso than I—and she knew all the things that needed to be done to make our Community Center, in particular, a place of welcoming beauty for my wedding to Jay.

Jay's four children, Nora, Lewey, Susan, and Rebekah, along with Lewey's wife, Joy, and their friends, Sue and Chuck Woodcock, came up from Georgia to witness the exchange of our vows.

My brother Paul and his wife, Kay, came down from Ontario, Canada, as well. As it happened, they stayed in the same area motel as Jay's girls and Kay, on hearing their Southern accent in the shared elevator, guessed that it was Jay's daughters. Later, they were introduced to each other at the wedding reception at Arbor Gate, the community in which I resided.

And since our wedding ceremony took place in December, Myerstown Baptist had been decorated beautifully for the Christmas season. Truly, everything fell into place. And as our senior pastor, the Reverend James Bitner, led us in the exchange of our vows, my heart bubbled over with joy and I began to weep.

Jay had taken my hand earlier and now he squeezed it for reassurance. Others, family and friends, were praying for me as well. This, coupled with a quick prayer to our Father above, enabled me to go on without further incident.

Our only disappointment for such a special time in my life was in that Michael, Kris and their three boys were unable to come up from N. Carolina. But I'll forever appreciate Michael's creative work in designing the lovely invitations for us and beautiful Church bulletins we had to hand out to our guests at the Ceremony.

CXCXCXCXCXCX

Now, with our first ten years (almost) behind us, I can say with confidence that a second marriage, or even a third[11], can be a beautiful thing if it's in the will of God and if He remains the focus of the couple's lives.

"Weeping may endure for a night, but joy comes in the morning" (Psa. 30:5).

And yes, there was an adjustment period. There always is, I would think, when you enter into a second or, as with Jay, a third marital relationship.[12]

But we have been able to talk out most of our frustrations and trust God to continue to be at work in our lives. Also, I have Diana to share with when I feel the need, and Jay his adult children.

They are all good listeners.

Not everybody would choose the route either of us chose at our age. But when you consider that so many widows and widowers live alone and are lonely, it's by far the better choice. Do I have any regrets? Perhaps one or two, the greater one being in that I had to leave my daughter, her family, my friends and my church behind. But where there is loss, there is also gain.

I've embraced a new culture, enjoyed meeting new people, become a great-grandmother and, more recently, with the birth of Cyrus James Tippins in 2021, a great-great-grandmother![13]

And, perhaps even more exciting for me, my grandson David and his wife, Kathleen, presented us with a new great-grandson, Reilly Francis, in December—just a few days before my birthday but exactly on his great-grandmother Ellen's birthday, December 19, 2021.

Jay continues to serve as interim or supply pastor when the need arises. He's also sorting through and giving away many of the books he's acquired over his years of ministry. At a time when many churches are disbanding their libraries in favor of online research, he feels there is still a need for handheld books for those who prefer to study that way, turning the pages by hand and highlighting as they go.

We are both of the same persuasion.

And, with Jay's encouragement, I have published two books and am working hard to complete my third by the end of this year, 2022.

Section III

Christian Growth

Chapter 8

A Life Lived For Jesus

Then those who feared the LORD talked with
each other, and the LORD listened and heard. A
scroll of remembrance was written in his presence concerning those who feared the LORD
and honored his name. Malachi 3:16

Some time back a friend who is now with the Lord called
with an invitation for me to spend the day with her.

"I'm planning a ride in the country," she enthused, "And I'd
love for you to come along."

"Just tell me where you plan to go and what time you think
we'll be home," I said. "I like to be here when Russ gets home
from work."

"Through Lancaster County[14]," she responded, cheerily.
"There's so much to see over that way and today looks as though
it would be a beautiful day to make a few stops in Paradise,
Bird-in-Hand, and Intercourse.

"And, too, she added, amiably, "There's a store I'm familiar with on the highway that sells handmade wicker baskets. I just love to go there. I think you would enjoy it, too!"

I thanked Diane and soon we were on our way.

Diane was a new friend, one whom I had bonded with almost immediately when we met at a weekly Bible study shortly after our family had returned to Pennsylvania from Washington State.

I was fortunate to meet Diane through our area coordinator for Friendship Bible Coffees.[15] Diane had actually called Sally, introducing herself as a new Christian wanting to connect with a group of ladies who were regularly studying the Bible.

I, too, had called Sally. I wanted to attend one of these groups as well as I had been involved in one in Washington State prior to our move.

The upshot of it was God had gone before and brought the three of us together. We met for the first time at Sally's home. After that, Diane and I continued to grow our friendship, mostly over the phone.

Diane had health issues but she didn't allow those to keep her from staying in touch with her friends. And having only recently given her *all* to Jesus Christ, she was hungry for relationships that would encourage her to grow in her faith.

Sally's Friendship Bible Coffee was not gathering during the summer months and Sally was not prepared to start it up again in the fall. She was studying for her master's degree in psychology; and with two small children at home, she was no longer able to take the time to prepare for or launch new Coffees at that time.

Although just returning to the area, (it had been 14 years since we'd lived in the Media area prior to our move to the

Pacific Northwest) and my family and I were just getting acclimated to our new neighborhood. This left me unprepared to lead a new Study, even if I had been asked, which I wasn't. And it was just as well. I soon became involved in a Christian Writers' group[16] and that would take a lot of my study time and some interaction weekly with a different group of ladies.

Diane was working parttime as assistant librarian at a well-known college in the area founded by Quakers. Additionally, starting out with only two or three of her college friends, Diane had only recently begun a *ministry* to the countless homeless in Philadelphia in the 1980s and 1990s.

Every Friday night during the cold winter months, she, Murray and Felix (both theology students) and a young woman from India (whose name I've forgotten), would take a sack full of peanut butter and jelly sandwiches they'd prepared and thermoses filled with hot drinks into the less desirable areas of the bustling city.

Keeping her compact car running, Murray, Felix and sometimes the young woman from India would politely approach any derelict they thought would be responsive. "So many are sick," Diane would tell me. "They are suffering from malnutrition, alcohol and drug abuse, living on the streets and in so many other ways."

"But aren't you afraid?" I asked her on several occasions. Both Russ and I admired her courage for it was something we felt we never could do. We did understand, of course, that we all have resources and spiritual gifts *if* we have a personal relationship with Jesus Christ. Diane was using hers creatively to bring some comfort to these men and women who found themselves in their hapless situation.[17]

After a long but satisfying day under blue skies and bright sunshine, Diane pulled in alongside the mailbox in front of my home.

We had chatted amiably as we drove along through the beautiful Pennsylvania farm country, not feeling pressured to talk but mostly just enjoying the scenery and one another's company.

Now, as Diane stopped the car and turned off the ignition, I caught a look of consternation on her face.

"Is something bothering you, Diane? I asked, a little hesitantly.

I waited, knowing she would open up if I gave her the opportunity to do so.

Finally, she asked, "Did you enjoy today?"

"Why, yes, Diane, I did. "It was fun. Our luncheon meal was delicious and I enjoyed my fellowship with you."

She paused. Then, choosing her words carefully, she said, "But…was it really *fellowship*? You know," she added, "When you stop to think about it, we talked about a lot of different things—*but* how much did we really include Jesus Christ in our conversation?"

I turned my head and caught a dancing sunbeam peeking through the towering oak near our mailbox. *She's right*, I thought. We had prayed briefly. But other than that, I had to agree that most of our conversation had been centered on ourselves.

"Diane," I confessed, "I'm ashamed to admit it, but what you say is true."

"I'm just a new Christian," my friend went on to say, "And I don't want you to think I don't appreciate my Christian friends."

"No, no, Diane," I affirmed, nodding my head in her direction.

"I, too, have experienced the same inner frustration when I've set aside a part of my day, wanting so much to share what God is doing in my life, and then having that excitement squelched by never-ending small talk."

"A few months ago," Diane continued, "I wouldn't have been so sensitive to this. But I've been studying the book of Acts, and one thing that's really impressed me is that the early church spent so much quality time together."

"Yes, Diane, that's true," I agreed. "And their fellowship was certainly centered on the Person of Jesus Christ. I'm thinking particularly of Acts 2:46 and 47, '*They worshiped together regularly at the Temple each day, met in small groups in homes for Communion, and shared their meals with great joy and thankfulness, praising God....*'" (The Living Bible).

We sat quietly for a moment, each with her own thoughts. Then, reaching over to touch her hand, I said a quick "*We'll be in touch*" and eased myself out of her small foreign car, thanking my friend for including me in her mini-excursion.

I knew Diane had given me something on which to ruminate. Evidently, I'd gotten used to staying politely within the conversational norms when the subject of religion came up. For someone who had loved to share her faith and sought out opportunities to do so, this was not a good sign.

I thanked the Holy Spirit for speaking to my heart and silently but resolutely asked him to forgive me for my insensitivity and to help me to be more alert on those occasions when I'm asked by a friend or acquaintance to join them for a day of refreshment.

Some may think that a life lived for Jesus is a wasted life. Certainly, there are things a Christ-follower chooses not to do because he fears it may mar his testimony. Such things, for instance, might be running with a fast crowd, hanging out in places that would give a bystander reason to believe he is not sincere about his faith, making wrong choices and giving in to temptation, spreading gossip about friends and acquaintances, and so on.

But living for Jesus brings much joy if we allow him to have his way in our lives.

Two years ago, 2020, brought with it the Coronavirus—a deadly virus which swept throughout the entire world bringing fear, sickness and death to many people, particularly our elderly.

It also brought with it the need to hunker down, as it were, removing ourselves from situations where we thought we might contract the virus and get horribly sick or die. This meant that church families, too, were required to practice social-distancing habits, the covering of our faces with masks, the endless washing of our hands and the things we touch, staying removed from locations where, because of crowds, we might be exposed to those who themselves were exposed and likely to get sick and most likely pass along the virus to others.

Through it, many of the faithful have chosen to stay away from church, either watching their own Services online or catching them later through the week.

An article in our local paper gave a report from one of the larger churches in our community. The pastor interviewed said his particular church had grown exponentially through going online with their weekly services, something they had already begun to do.

"Online views went from 200 to 2,000 per Sunday, reaching all over the U.S., Guatemala, Europe and Haiti," he said. "COVID-19 has made Eastside's online services a vessel for global outreach."[18]

And while they have since started up again and now, as before, meet in their church building for their regular service and activities, undoubtedly they will continue to live-stream for their growing viewing audience far into the future.

Chapter 9

Anger, a Privilege?

He that is slow to anger is better than the mighty;
and he that ruleth his spirit than he that taketh a
city. Proverbs 16:32, KJV.

It was a bright, sunny day in mid-July. The ice-cold lemonade my friend Elizabeth and I shared in the warmth of her attractive pink and white living room refreshed me.

We'd touched on several topics in conversation—Elizabeth's new rug, her son Billy's college classes, and the renovation of their home at the Shore.

But Elizabeth was restless and I sensed she wanted to discuss something of greater importance. I waited. Finally, she said, "Diana…you seem so happy all the time. Are you really as happy as you appear to be?"

I paused shortly to reflect on what she'd said, then replied, "Yes, most of the time I am, Elizabeth."

"But…don't you get angry or cranky or sad?"

"Of course I do!" I laughed. "But I try not to dwell on things that are going to make me feel that way."

Elizabeth had been a professing Christian all her life. She went to church regularly and appeared to be devout in her faith. She had committed her life to Jesus Christ and recently we'd completed a home Bible study course with her. The learning sessions often focused on problems that Christians encounter from day to day.

"Elizabeth, God's Word is real! It's alive and active. His Word, together with his Holy Spirit, helps us to live above our circumstances and to control our emotions and negative thought patterns."

"That sounds great in theory," she countered skeptically. "But a little impracticable—at least, for me. I tend to be high-strung and emotional and, unfortunately, I react before I think."

Elizabeth went on to relate a recent incident in which their fifteen-year-old son, Billy, had asked for and received permission from his parents to stay home rather than to accompany them to their summer home at the shore on a particular weekend.

The understanding had been that he would not have any friends over while his parents were away.

Billy betrayed this trust by inviting a few of his closest friends to an impromptu party. Later, when Elizabeth heard about it through one of the mothers, she was furious. After venting her anger, her retaliation had been to give Billy the silent treatment for several days.

"Lucky for me," Elizabeth said, "my husband is a very controlled and even-tempered man. He was able to talk with Billy about his disobedience and, together, they decided on Billy's discipline.

"But," she continued, "Why couldn't I have handled it more sensibly? Why did I have to sputter like a wet hen before I had chance to talk it over with my husband?"

"Elizabeth," I admonished gently, "perhaps you're being too hard on yourself. Temperament and upbringing have a lot to do with the way we handle our emotions, you know."

"But, somehow I don't think you'd react that way?"

"Ummm...sometimes I may. But I've discovered that by hiding God's Word in my heart, together with the Holy Spirit's nudging, has given me the help I need to keep me from becoming ballistic.

Another thing I've learned that's been helpful to me, too, is that anger, in itself, is not sin. It's when we give in to it that it becomes sin.

"I can recall one incident in which my husband Russ and I were getting ready to leave for a trip across the country. We were to drive up from Washington State to Vancouver, Canada, stay overnight with my brother Al, and then leave by plane the next morning for Nova Scotia.

"While loading the car, my husband made some silly remark that didn't sit right with me. And, rather than confront him with it, I gave the garage door a good swift kick. 'Owwww!' I yelled, hopping with pain! I can feel it yet!"

"It soon became apparent that I'd either badly sprained my foot or had fractured my ankle. But rather than delay our trip, I chose to make the flight. When we arrived in Nova Scotia, I got medical attention immediately. X-rays confirmed my fears. It was a fracture! This meant I was forced to spend the entire four weeks of our vacation with my foot and leg in a cast!

"That taught me a good lesson, Elizabeth, and has helped me to remember that in allowing myself the *privilege* of becoming angry, I may have to suffer the consequences!"

Elizabeth nodded. "Well, I'm sure glad to hear you still have problems, too! I was beginning to wonder if I was different," she chuckled.

"Well, you are unique, but not different," I teased. Each of us struggles with things of this sort. But it *is* encouraging to know we're not in this struggle alone.

"By remembering, too, that God really does care about all the minuscule things that happen to us, that He really is in control of our lives, enables us to draw on His strength and to not rely on our own human resources."

"Tell you what!" I suggested, getting up to leave, "Let's make a pact to pray for each other regularly. I'll pray that God will help you to be less explosive in your anger, and you pray for me that God will help me to release my anger in a positive way."

"I like that idea!" she agreed, showing me to the door.

As I climbed into my son's compact car and eased myself out onto the road that led to our home, a Scripture verse surfaced in my spirit:

> *Praise be to the God and Father of our Lord Jesus Christ, the Father of compassion and the God of all comfort, who comforts us in all our troubles, so that we can comfort those in any trouble with the comfort we ourselves receive from God.* (2 Corinthians 1:3-4, NIV) (Emphasis, mine.)

Chapter 10

Confrontation

If your brother or sister sins against you, rebuke
them; and if they repent, forgive them. (Luke
17:3, NIV.)

A recent exchange of words with a difficult neighbor once
again reminded me of the importance of confrontation in
resolving differences.

In our three years in the neighborhood, my husband, Russ,
and I had overlooked Leslie and Pete's constant nitpicking over,
what seemed to us, inconsequential matters. We had listened
politely as they complained about other neighbors, reminding
ourselves how fortunate we were that we, at least, got along
with them—if only on a superficial plane.

But when Leslie called on Christmas Eve to grumble that
she could hear the Christmas carols playing on our stereo, I
smarted! Of course, I reasoned, she is Jewish. If indeed she
could hear our stereo, the carols heralding Christ's birth would
offend her. "But we live here too!" I complained aloud to Russ.
Nonetheless, I immediately turned off the stereo and retired

to the family room to join my husband in watching a television special.

Now, several weeks later, Leslie was calling to apologize. "I'm home with the flu," she said, "and I have had time to think. I am sorry I was cross with you."

Leslie went on to say she knew once spring arrived and she saw me out in the backyard, she would feel bad that she couldn't say "hello."

Confrontation is never easy. Apologizing was not easy for Leslie, but she valued my friendship more than her own pride.

Jesus knew the importance of confrontation. In Matthew 18:15 He said, *"If your brother or sister sins, go and point out their fault, just between the two of you." (Emphasis, mine.)*

If more of us would heed this advice, I'm convinced we would see fewer church splits, divorces, and severed relationships in families.

Howard Hendricks says, "Too often I have seen marriages go down the drain, relationships deteriorate to the point of destruction, people with glaring personal limitations go unchecked—all because Christians who know precisely what is wrong will not love sufficiently to address the problem."

Scripture tells us, "Whoever rebukes a person will in the end gain favor...." (Proverbs 28:23, NIV).

Rebuke, if given in the right spirit, will often bring healing to a relationship. Many people feel that the mature way to handle a quarrel is to ignore the problem rather than to initiate a confrontation. But that only builds barriers.

Sometimes God must override dissension to accomplish His purposes. Scripture relates an incident where Paul and Barnabus, two missionary giants, engaged in an argument. Barnabus wanted his cousin John Mark to accompany them as they visited the churches. Paul said, "No!" John Mark had deserted them on an earlier mission and Paul undoubtedly felt that Mark lacked the character to complete the task at hand.

The outcome of the quarrel was that Barnabus took Mark and left for Cyprus, and Paul took Barnabas and journeyed to Syria and Cilicia. They accomplished two missionary journeys rather than one. While Barnabus is not mentioned again in the Book of Acts, Paul later speaks of Barnabus as an ally. The two, despite their dissension, evidently remained friends throughout their lives.

Sometimes to avoid confrontation we simply withdraw. The Joneses and Smiths have a rousing agreement over finances at their church's quarterly business meeting. One couple feels that the pastor deserves a raise in salary. The other couple maintains any further *faith* giving should be extended to the Browns on the mission field.

Finally, after a heated debate, the Joneses win the argument, but it ends the warm relationship they once shared with the Smiths. Both parties still converse, but their disagreement has created a barrier. Confrontation, with reconciliation in mind, would restore the relationship the couples once enjoyed and set a positive example for the church.

Jesus gives sound advice in Luke 17:3-4:

> *"So watch yourselves. If your brother or sister sins against you, rebuke them; and if they repent, forgive them. Even if they sin against you seven times in a day and seven times come back to you saying 'I repent,' you must forgive them." (NIV, Emphasis mine.)*

Rebuke and forgive. No passing over or pretending a problem does not exist, but rather confrontation and forgiveness for this is biblical.

When Leslie called to seek my forgiveness, the sincerity of her plea melted my anger. My rebuke was gentle. My forgiveness, I trust, was Christ-like. Our desire to build a solid, lasting relationship made confrontation and forgiveness a little easier for us both.

Chapter 11

Divine Appointments - Charles

He [Jesus] looked up and said to him, "Zacchaeus, come down immediately. I must stay at your house today." So he came down at once and welcomed him gladly. Luke 19:5-6 (NIV)

All of us have what some call *divine appointments*—those special occasions when, seemingly out of the blue, someone will come into our lives. These may be people we once knew, an acquaintance we'd met somewhere, or a long-lost relative, but they're people God knows needs some *Tender Loving Care* and He brings us back together—if only for a short time.

My nephew Charles[19] was one of these.

A severe concussion earlier in the year left him no longer able to perform his job as stunt man in the movie industry.

Money was tight. Bills were outstanding.

Additionally, he was suffering from depression and his medication did not seem to be working.

As we chatted on Social media, I remembered that Charles had made a decision for Christ as a child. I asked him if he recalled that decision.

Without hesitation he assured me that he had and that he prayed to God every day. "I know I'm still a child of God," he said, confidently.

Over the course of the next few weeks we continued to visit through the media. In time I suggested he seek out a church for fellowship and ministerial counsel. I also suggested he talk to his dad—whom he had tried to talk to before on several occasions but *"got nowhere,"* he said.

I took this to mean that Donald was leaving it up to Charles to find his own solution to his problem.

I urged him to try again, and he did—to no avail.

With Charles's permission, I called his father. We'd always had a good relationship and I wanted to hear what he had to say.

Not surprisingly, I discovered that Don's perspective was different from Charles'. He assured me that he had *been there* for Charles, supporting him in multiple ways for several years.

Recently, he had to tell Charles that he could no longer support him financially. Now retired at 72 and living in a small townhome in an expensive area of a particular city, he and Nancy needed all they had to get along.

After assuring Charles that I hadn't said anything his dad could take offense to, he responded with, "That's good; I don't need any more problems."

Six months went by and I didn't hear anything from Charles. I knew better than to call Don again, but Jay and I kept Charles in our prayers.

I also knew in my heart of hearts that God had a purpose for bringing him into my life at this time. He was only a boy when we moved back east so my contact with him had been sporadic over the years.

He grew up without my ever getting to know him as an adult. Now I felt I was experiencing a *divine encounter.*

Paul, in his letter to the Ephesians, urged the saints there to *"be kind to one another, tender-hearted, forgiving one another even as Christ forgave them" (Eph. 4:32).* So I knew what I had to do.

Six months went by and one day when I was working in the yard, my cell phone jangled. I didn't recognize the number but I answered anyway. "Hello," I said, a bit guardedly.

"Hi, Aunt Diane," the voice on the other end said warmly, "It's me, Charles."

"Well hello, Charles," I responded cheerily, surprised to hear from my nephew. "How are you?"

"I'm fine," he said, his slight inflection giving away the area of the country in which he lived, "I just wanted to thank you for helping me out when you did."

He went on to share how, since then, he'd gotten a part in a television series that looked promising, he was able to pay the rent on his apartment, and he had completed his studies at university.

I breathed a silent *thank you* to my heavenly Father.

"Charles, I am so happy for you," I cried sincerely.

We concluded our conversation with a promise from Charles that, when he could get far enough ahead financially to make the trip, he would come to see us.

We ended our call and, after pausing for a few minutes to regain my composure, I walked swiftly across the yard to tell Jay my good news.

Whether or not I hear from Charles again soon is an unknown, but he knows I love him and that I'm being supportive of him as best I can from a distance.

My prayer is that, in the long run, this will point him back to God, if it hasn't already.

It was love that brought the prodigal son home. Perhaps it will be my love that will bring Charles back to God.

Chapter 12

Generational Friendships

A friend loves at all times, and a brother is born
for a time of adversity. *(Proverbs 17:17, NIV)*

I was on Social Media, checking out several of my friends'
posts, when I was alerted to a new message coming in on
Messenger. Curious, I checked it out. To my surprise and
delight, it was from one of Michael and Diana's childhood
friends, Will Brady.[20]

Will and his family live in the Pacific Northwest. When
Will and his two siblings were growing up, I taught each of the
three in turn in Sunday school as they passed through 1st and
2nd grades.

I'd had no connection with any of the family since returning
to the East Coast in 1982, although we had seen the parents on
at least one occasion when revisiting the area.

We heard, of course, news of the children as they, along
with ours, grew up and moved on with their lives. Will had
chosen to attend a conservative Bible college in mid-western

Canada to complete his education. While there, he met his wife-to-be, Alicia.

They went on to have four children.

Will's sister, Angela, after completing her education and with her parents' blessing, chose full-time mission work where she met and married her husband, Carl.l Angela gave birth to three children. Sadly, without warning, Carl passed away in his sleep and Angela was left to raise their three beautiful children on her own.

As I later found out from Will, Angela came back home where, together with her parents, Steve and Marlene, as well as Angela's siblings, she raised the children in the Christian faith.

The youngest of Will and Angela's siblings, Kynlee, a teacher, has remained in the community in which both the parents and Will and Angela reside.

The whole family, Will shared with me as we chatted on several subsequent occasions, live in a communal setting in which he and his sisters grew up.

I did recall Steve, a successful carpenter, building a large addition to their home in the late '70's when Russ and I and Michael and Diana were still living in the area.

Actually, we had been in the home the once when they had a housewarming on completion of the remodeling. The expanded area made for a beautiful roomy interior for holding various young peoples' activities, which was the intent of the project.

Steve later built a smaller home on the property for Marlene's mother and dad to live in as they aged. This later became Steve and Marlene's home, making room for Will and Angela to move into the main house.

Kynlee, I understand, lives in another area of the community.

Not every family would be happy with this arrangement because of the proximity of the living quarters but, knowing this family, I was not surprised to learn that, for them, this became a workable arrangement.

From our observation, all members of this family are easy-going and amicable.

And, too, the property is in a beautiful country environment. I don't recall if there's a lake on the property itself; but, if not, there is a large one nearby. I personally have not seen it since the visit I mentioned above, but I know the lake itself would have, over time, drawn many to build in that particular area.

The Brady's were a special family to all of us in the late '60's through to the early '80's when we lived in the Pacific Northwest as both Will and his sister, Angela, were two of Michael and Diana's closest friends. Kynlee, of course, was younger and still a preteen when we moved away.

In the early 70's, the parents, too, like Russ and me, were young in the faith, and while our paths crossed only at church, we—moreso at a distance than close up—appreciated the combined interest we shared in raising our children in a *believers'* environment.

For me, it was exciting to reconnect with Will and get *caught up* with his family's happenings since I had last seen and talked with the Brady family.

Our conversations became, as would be expected, that of one adult to another and no longer the adult-to-child relationship—Will having grown up, married and having children and, more recently, grandchildren of his own.

This meant I could speak to him of my own children's children (mine and Russ' grandchildren) and of their accomplishments. I knew, too, that Will and Michael chatted occasionally on Social media and I knew as well that Angela and Diana had touched base at least once or twice in recent years.

All this is to say that, sometimes, friendships and/or relationships come full circle.

While our circumstances change over the years, and people move about, the impact a person makes on one's life is always there. If given the opportunity to revisit the past and that past has been a positive experience, the friendship will reignite and both parties will be the better for it.

I have seen this happen on several occasions in my own life, through little or no effort of my own.

One *first* cousin, for instance, Peter, along with his wife, Stella, became very near and dear to me after my dad's demise in 1982.

Although Dad died in February in Vancouver, Canada, and a memorial service was held for him there, his ashes later were placed at the foot of his father's grave in Hubbards, Nova Scotia.

Peter and Stella, along with several other members on both sides of the family, attended the brief graveside service that day. This, then, was when my friendship with Peter and my dad's side of the family really took root.

I should explain here, too, that with travel being what it was back in the forties and fifties, my siblings and I hadn't seen, as children, our close relatives more than perhaps a dozen times over the years. At least, not that I can remember.

And while we *loved* each other, our friendships hadn't had the opportunity to establish deep roots.

But, that day, on that occasion, we came together in a new spirit. Sharing a delicious meal at a beautiful Inn overlooking the golf course, enjoying the camaraderie of next of kin, we formed a new bond, a new relationship that would begin, figuratively, at Day One.

And while time and distance continue to limit our on-site, get-together times, cards and emails keep us close in spirit. For this, I am grateful.

I've often wondered, as I read and reread the gospel accounts, how Jesus' disciples related to each other on a daily basis. We're familiar with the consternation shown by several of the men when James and John, at the urging of their mother, prodded Jesus to assign them the most important positions in His kingdom which was yet to come.

Humility—at that time at least—was not something that was innate in these two brothers.

We see this especially in John where, often, he describes himself as *"the one whom Jesus loved."* (John 13:24.) (Emphasis, mine.) Perhaps, being Jesus' *first* cousin, he enjoyed a certain affinity with his Master that the others had not attained. At least, not yet.

We know that the disciples as well recognized this familial bond John enjoyed, for as they share the Passover Meal together, Peter nudges John to ask Jesus which of them will betray him (v. 24, NIV).

John, unabashedly, leans in toward Jesus and says, "Lord, who is it?"

Jesus answered, "It is the one to whom I will give this piece of bread when I have dipped it in the dish (v. 26, NIV)."

Jesus then proceeds to dip the bread and to pass it to Judas.

To be honest, the familial bond I have always experienced with my *first* cousins isn't there quite so much with others in the family to whom I'm related. Perhaps what we see in John, even moreso than in James, is a relationship that has come about through their mothers' sisterhood by birth.

The two Marys are both seen at the cross of Christ. And later, Mary, Jesus' mother, is specifically mentioned as being with the women and Jesus' brothers in the upper room as they await the promised coming of the Holy Spirit. "They all joined together constantly in prayer, *along with the women and Mary the mother of Jesus*, and with his brothers" (Acts 1:14, NIV).

We would assume, then, that Jesus' Aunt Mary would be at her sister's side here as she was at the cross when Jesus suffered and, ultimately, died and yielded up His Spirit to God.

Another familial bonding among Jesus' disciples was Peter and Andrew. Both were fishermen and the sons of their father, Zebedee. Obviously, their temperaments and personalities were quite different. Peter was the impetuous type, while Andrew came across as one who was willing to give himself over to his brother's leadership.

These four, James and John and Peter and Andrew, had the commonality of a shared livelihood. They were all commercial fishermen. Jesus chose these men, not because of their livelihood or their personality traits or their familial bond, but because of what He planned to do through them.

He would be spending several years with them, both day and night, and instructing them in areas that would prepare them for ministry, not only then but later on when He was no longer with them in the physical sense.

The latter would be when, through them, He would build his Church.

Knowing this, Jesus explained to them their need to stay close to each other and to love one another.

The Scriptures record him as saying, "A new command I give you: Love one another. As I have loved you, so you must love one another. By this everyone will know that you are my disciples, if you love one another" (John 13:34-35, NIV).

Love, then as now, demonstrates to unbelievers that Jesus' followers have *internalized* God's message of love. It would be that which would grow his church and hold it together in times of persecution.

Even as it does today.

Section IV

Family Togetherness

Chapter 13

Tommy

Jesus said, "Let the little children come to me, and do not hinder them, for the kingdom of heaven belongs to such as these." Matthew 19:14, NIV.

To entertain him, I challenged my 9-year-old grandson[21] to a game of I Spy while we waited for his mother to come out of the grocery store.

I looked around the parking lot and saw very little other than a sea of vehicles, most of which were the standard black, white, dark blues and greens.

"I spy with my little eye," I said, squinting as I tried to determine which color car or truck would be the most challenging to spot, "Something that is forest green."

Tommy quickly looked around and spotting a green car, he exclaimed: "That one?"

"That's the one," I said, acknowledging his enthusiastic response with a nod and a smile. "Now it's your turn."

And so we took a couple of turns but Tommy quickly tired of the game.

"Tell you what," I said, not wanting my lively and inquisitive grandson to suffer boredom, "Let's play a word game. I'll give you a sentence with a *blank* word in it and you fill in the blank."

"No, I'm not good at words," the eight-year-old responded, half-heartedly.

"Sure you are," I said, perhaps a little too enthusiastically. "Here's one for you: The trip to Grandma's house was *blank* and a little tedious."

"*Boring*," was Tommy's quick retort.

"I actually meant *slow*," I countered, "But that's okay. It certainly could be *boring*.

"Now you give me one."

"No, I don't want to," he said, uncovering a ball of play dough and squishing it between his fingers.

"Okay," I agreed. "How about sharing?"

Without hesitation, he pulled apart the pliable, putty-like material and handed me a sizeable piece to work with.

Quickly and with little thought to the end result, I worked the soft green ball into something that quite surprisingly resembled a foot.

I passed it back to Tommy and, smiling mischievously, said, "Here's Big Foot."

Tommy laughed aloud in spite of himself.

I thought he would immediately squish them both, but he didn't. In fact, he was still holding *the foot* when we pulled into the driveway at home.

Like most grandmothers, I cherish those times when I can be with my grandchildren. But busy schedules, school, extra-curricular activities and just the busyness of every-day living makes it hard for the parents to find time for company, sometimes even if it's their mom.

These same busy schedules make it difficult, too, for those same parents to break away and drive some distance to visit their loved ones. The days of *over the river and through the woods to Grandmother's house we go* are a thing of the past. More realistically, grandmas, and grandpas too, have to take the initiative to travel if they are to spend time with their grandchildren.

But love is a great common denominator. Cards, phone calls on special days, and nightly prayers are all ways of maintaining that all-important connection that keep the fires of love aflame.

I'll never forget what Nannie Warner, my husband's mom, said to me on one of the several occasions she visited in our home: *"Enjoy them now. These are the best years of your life."*

Unfortunately, parents of young children tend to be short-sighted. And with good reason. When your three-year-old has been playing in a mud puddle out front while you are busily clearing up the lunch dishes and your five-year-old is busily trying to strangle her, somehow you can't envisage a time when you will be able to sit down—alone—with a second cup of coffee and meditate from your cherished book, the Bible.

But it happens and all too quickly. Then you realize that, as you read your Bible and finish your second cup of coffee, there won't be anyone coming home from school, kicking off his or her soiled sneakers just inside the front door, and calling out: "Hi, Mom. I'm home."

There will just be the silence. And, of course, the memories. They are always with you. Good and not so good.

I guess that's what Nannie Warner meant when she said what she said that day. Perhaps her memories were not as sweet as she would have liked them to be. Perhaps she had her regrets. Admittedly, I have some, too.

Most of us do, in one way or another.

But loving our children and then having to go it alone without them is all part of the cycle of life.

They too will experience some quiet, reflective days as well as, one by one, their children go off to college, choose their life mates, and move on with their lives.

In the meantime, there's nothing wrong with being a little sentimental as long as we don't dwell too much on the past.

Life presents its challenges at every stage.

Embracing it is the key, not only to survival, but to growth. Wherever *we* are in *our* life-cycle, we need to give it all we have. Be the best we can be. Enjoy our alone times but make a life outside our walls as well. Cast off our concerns and do some of those things we've wanted to do but never took time to.

As a wise wag once said, "Go for the gusto!"

It's good advice. I'm still working on it and hope to be until I'm taken home to Glory. In this regard, I'm reminded of a particular hymn that's been around for many years. I'd like to share it with you:

What a Day That Will Be[22]

There is coming a day when no heartaches shall come,
No more clouds in the sky,
No more tears to dim the eye;
All is peace forevermore on that happy golden shore,
What a day glorious day that will be.

Chorus

What a day that will be when my Jesus I shall see,
And I look upon His face, the One who saved me by
His grace;
When He takes me by the hand, and leads me through the
Promised Land,
What a day, glorious day that will be.
There'll be no sorrow there, no more burdens to bear,
No more sickness, no pain, no more parting over there;
And forever I will be with the One who died for me,
What a day glorious day that will be.

Chapter 14

Plant a Tree, Save the Planet

"Blessed...is the one whose delight is in the law of the LORD, and who meditates on his law day and night. That person is like a tree planted by streams of water, which yields its fruit in season...whatever they do prospers."[23] (Psalms 1:1-3, Journal the Word, NIV)

As a past member of the Arbor Day Foundation, I'm always interested in reading current articles in their journal about members who have made an outstanding contribution to conservation and wildlife protection. In one of their back issues, for instance, CEO John Rosenow wrote about Stewart Udall, Interior Secretary during the 1960s, and his dedication to the earth's preservation.

"Under his authority," Rosenow wrote, "four national parks, six national monuments and dozens of national recreation areas, historic sites and wildlife refuges were created. Udall helped secure passage of the Wilderness Act, Land and Water

Conservation Fund Act, Endangered Species Act, and National Historic Preservation Act."

"A product of the arid West," states Rosenow, "Stewart never took trees for granted."

Raised in Atlantic Canada where trees are plentiful and appreciated for their contribution to the economy as well as to wildlife preservation, Russ was forever planting trees where we lived. On one property alone, he planted over one hundred trees, and these were not seedlings. Most were four to six feet tall. It was not an easy task but, for him, it was rewarding and enjoyable.

Prior to a recent move, our son Michael was doing the same thing. On his "bare" acre in North Carolina, he planted 75 to 100 trees in five to ten years, along with flowering shrubs and perennials. Because of the long, hot, dry summers there, he would lose one now and then. But because of his dogged determination, he and Kris and the three boys saw and enjoyed much fruit for his labor.

Many of us, of course, no longer have large properties on which to plant trees nor are we physically able to do so. But that does not mean we cannot contribute in some way to keeping our land green for future generations.

Occasionally I will order the specimen featured in the current Arbor Day circular and have it sent to one of my family's homes. It comes as a surprise to them and I am rewarded in two ways: first, in their delight, and second, in knowing I have done something to keep America green. Granted, my contribution may be small. But multiplied many times over, it amounts to a lot.

In a way, it's like corporate prayer. Although God hears each of his children's prayers, spoken or unspoken, corporate prayer has multiplied power.

The same goes for giving.

A wise Christian lady once told me when I was apologizing for our being able to send only a small monthly amount to her missionary family abroad that if we gave what we could and someone else gave what they could, God would multiply it and her family's needs would be met.

This was evidently true for her family was on the mission field for over 20 years.

It's a principle I took to heart and I continue to be challenged by it to this day.

Trees[24]
Alfred Joyce Kilmer

I think that I shall never see
A poem [as] lovely as a tree.
A tree whose hungry mouth is prest
Against the earth's sweet flowing breast;
A tree that looks at God all day,
And lifts her leafy arms to pray;
A tree that may in Summer wear
A nest of robins in her hair;
Upon whose bosom snow has lain;
Who intimately lives with rain.

Chapter 15

Alligators!

He [Jesus] said [to his disciples who had fished all night and caught nothing], "Throw your net on the right side of the boat and you will find some." When they did, they were unable to haul the net in because of the large number of fish."
John 21:6, NIV.

We live on a beautiful piece of property. It's beautiful in part because we work on it a lot of the time.

It's also beautiful because God blesses the work of our hands.

When I first moved south after marriage to Jay just over nine years ago, I wondered if I could endure the insufferable heat of the Georgia summers.

Coupled with the heat were the swarms of gnats waiting to dive bomb you when you went to and from the mail box.

There were also the monstrous cockroaches that lived in the grass and in cardboard storage boxes, and occasionally, in your house as well.

But perhaps the worst little critters I had to get used to were the ugly green tree frogs that come out at dusk and cling to your windows at night; the possums that forage for food in the wee hours of the morning; the armadillos, *aka anteaters*, as well as the moles and voles that leave trails through your flower beds, searching for grubs to satiate their insufferable appetites.

To be honest, I was just beginning to tolerate the gnats and mosquitoes when Jay said, *"We'll soon be getting the Love Bugs. They come about July every year."*

"Love Bugs!" I exclaimed. "What on earth are Love Bugs?"

He laughed. "They're called that because they copulate in the air. They lay their eggs in the grass, then they die. They won't hurt you but they make a mess of your grill and your windshield as you're pushing sixty going down the road."

"Good grief!" I said. "What next?"

"Well," he responded, "You haven't seen any alligators yet."

"Alligators? No, and I don't want to. Where are the alligators? Are there any around here?"

"I don't think so," he responded cheerily, obviously enjoying my look of consternation. "But they used to have them over in one of the parks not far from here. I heard they took them all out. We'll take a ride over there one day and check it out.

"But first I want to fix up our dinghy so we can do some fishing."

"I can hardly wait," I mused aloud while pondering silently, *"I wonder what I've gotten myself into!"*

But knowing how important it was to Jay, and looking forward to a new experience, I watched with interest as he replaced the old seats with new, repainted the boat, and rummaged around until he found life vests for both of us.

Finally, the day arrived. I put together a box lunch for each of us, donned a warm vest as the day was cool, and patiently guided Jay as he hooked up the boat to the SUV.

The park he had in mind was perhaps ten miles from our home so, coupled with our anticipation to put the boat in the water and trawl our fishing lines, the ride too was enjoyable.

When we passed the first pond, there were a few motorized boats on the water but not many, maybe three or four.

A park ranger was visible near the entrance. He didn't stop us. And even if he had, we had our fishing licenses.

Jay had thought of everything.

Soon we passed a second pond and a nice picnic area with tables and benches.

"How far are we going?" I asked Jay.

"Not much farther," he said. "We're almost there."

I wondered why we weren't seeing many people or vehicles. I did notice the dirt road was becoming narrower and, other than meeting a service truck, there didn't seem to be anyone on the road.

Then the third pond came into view and it was such a beautiful spot. I took note and mentioned to Jay that the area belonged to a particular club and was obviously used by them for target practice.

"But it's also open to the public," he assured me.

Considering it was such a beautiful day, I wondered why there was only one other couple who had readied their rods and reels for fishing. Their truck camper was nearby.

The pond was still and blue, as blue as a kitten's eyes at birth.

Other than the open area owned by the aforementioned club and a public fishing dock, trees surrounded the pond.

I drank in the beauty of the place, thinking how much I'd missed for so many years not living on or near the fresh water.

Jay expertly backed the boat down into the water while I guided him as best I could. Then, parking the SUV, we pushed off from the dock and he trawled while I opened our lunch boxes.

The sun warmed our faces as, together, we enjoyed our sandwiches, sodas and chips and thanked God aloud for giving us such a pretty day in which to share our time together.

Casually, while trying not to talk too loud so we wouldn't scare any fish that might be nearby, I asked Jay, *"Have you ever seen a real live alligator? You know, other than in a protected area?"*

Jay grinned, pointing across the lake. "Look over there," he said, "You see that head sticking up out of the water?"

I stared in the direction where he pointed.

"Oh, my gosh!" I said. "Why didn't you tell me there were alligators here?"

"I didn't know," he said. To this day, I want to believe he was telling the truth.

"Let's get out of here!" I cried. "Lord, please help us. I don't want to be eaten by an alligator!"

Jay, evidently, didn't either as, together, we reeled in our fishing lines and, each using an oar, paddled speedily back to the dock.

Once safely ashore, we sent up a prayer of thanks to God for keeping us safe in what might have been a life or death situation. We later learned that there were as many as eighteen alligators in that particular pond. And, no, they hadn't been removed.[25]

Chapter 16

Death in my Garden

"Are not two sparrows sold for a penny? Yet not one of them will fall to the ground outside your Father's care. And even the very hairs of your head are all numbered. So don't be afraid; you are worth more than many sparrows." Matthew 10:29-31, NIV, Journal the Word Bible.

J ay stood at my side as I rinsed the dinner dishes and loaded the dishwasher.

Casually he remarked, "A cat just caught one of your birds."

He said what he said so matter-of-factly that I scarcely looked up. But when I did, Oh my, I barely caught glimpse of a triumphant Tabby proudly strutting away — not running, mind you, but S-T-R-U-T-T-I-N-G away with one of our beautiful Cardinals in its mouth.

Dropping my tea towel on the dryer rack, I ran to the patio door and yelled, *"Shoo, Cat. Get out of here!"* Tom Cat quickly dropped his prize and leaped and ran around the corner of the house—presumably, across the yard and back to wherever he came from.

"Oh, I can't believe it," I moaned to Jay, *"Don't tell me we're going to have cats lurking around here, hunting down our birds."*

Jay spoke up. "Well, I don't remember seeing this particular one before. And, other than the two or three kittens that were dropped off, I haven't seen any on the property at all."

Both Jay and I loved the birds. Jay had built a number of bluebird boxes and screwed three of them to several posts he had erected in several different spots in both the front and back yards.

He'd given the rest away.

He'd also taken particular care to cover the feeding area over the hanging feeders located off the back porch so the seed would stay dry when it rained. The overhead shelter also provided some visual protection from the hawks that fly overhead.

Then, for at least four years, we'd watched and prayed that the Purple Martins would find the gourds he'd taken pains to clean out and paint, readying them for nesting when the beautiful purple-black birds came back to the area in the spring of the year.

We were finally rewarded when, three years ago, we spotted two scouts checking out the gourds and, quite possibly, our general surroundings for safety and protection. Two weeks later, more of them arrived, and, as we watched from a distance, the friendly birds flew in and out of the prepared gourds, high, high overhead—swooping and diving—then down, down into the circular openings that were the doorways to what would become their nests.

There were sixteen birds in all, two to a nest. We figured at two little ones to a nest, there would be eight in all. How many of them, we wondered, would come back the next year? And, if they did come back, how many would be the little ones who had become mature? And how many would be from the original sixteen?

Of course, we had no way of knowing, but it was fun and somewhat educational to watch their habits as they seemed to take turns guarding the gourds, flying off during the day—presumably searching for food to bring back to the little ones—and finally, returning at mid-day and again at dusk to settle down for the night.

Birds and other small creatures, such as rabbits, feel quite safe in our environment because we don't have dogs or cats. Also, most of our yard is quite open.

And while there are numerous tall pines and flowering shrubs all around our home, predators could feel exposed and vulnerable.

Deer do come out at night to feed on ripened fruit in season.

We've also spotted foxes, possibly twins, on one occasion, and a bobcat off to the edge of the woods on several occasions. The bobcat is much larger than a housecat and looks somewhat fearsome. It unnerves me a bit, but Jay says you'd never be able to get near him because he'd run.

He needn't worry. I'd run first, if I spied him first!

There are large birds of prey, too, such as hawks and owls, that are always swooping high overhead. Occasionally, they will dive down very low in our yard, checking out either mice on the run, or perhaps a stray rat or snake moving quickly through the grass.

These make me a little anxious and, last year, we lost a mockingbird that seemed to think I was its mother.

It's true. He did think I was his mother. Let me tell you why I think this.

Both Jay and I were at our computers one morning in our home office and we heard this rather insistent, *tap, tap* on the window.

Jay heard it first. I guess I was deeply engrossed in what I was doing.

"Look!" he said, "There's a bird at the window. He seems to be trying to get your attention!"

Jay is a tease so, at first, I thought he was just trying to get a rise out of me.

"Well," I said, rather skeptically, "I doubt that, Jay. He's probably seeing his reflection in the window and wants to make friends with the "other" bird."

We ignored the tap, tapping for awhile, thinking the bird would go away.

He didn't.

For several hours that morning, he moved from one window to the next as I moved from one room to the next.

Finally, I opened the door in the living room, making sure the storm door was locked so the bird couldn't gain entry. Then, and only then, did it seem to take note and flew away.

This went on, off and on, for about two weeks. Then we went away for a fortnight. When we returned, I went outside one morning to check on my flower garden and I was alerted to the most beautiful singing in the trees.

Honestly, it seemed heaven-sent. The trills and notes were so melodic and captivating, I could not help but stop and listen.

I knew it had to be *my* mockingbird! I also knew it had to be happy. No creature could sing like that if it were not happy.

Then one beautiful Sunday afternoon, Jay's son, Lewey, and his lovely wife, Joy, stopped by to visit. The *tap, tapping* started up again. To be honest, I didn't even notice it—I'd grown used to it, you see—until Joy brought it to my attention.

From where she and Lewey sat, they could see the bird at the living room window.

"Oh," I said nonchalantly with a wave of my hand, "He pecks at the window for hours on end. He thinks I'm his mother," I added a little sheepishly.

Getting up from my chair, I opened the door where the bird could see us and, like before, he pecked at the glass storm door a couple of times, then flew away.

One morning not long after that, Jay came in from outdoors with a large feather in his hand.

I think something got your mockingbird, he said.

"Oh, no!" I exclaimed.

While I hadn't always appreciated the tapping and pecking on the windows, I did feel a certain affinity with the bird and I certainly didn't wish it any harm!

I ran out where Jay said he found the feather and, sure enough, it looked like there had been a scuffle. Jay had been gracious to bring the one feather he picked up to me.

Sadly, I studied the large, grey feather—the remains of my friend. Later, rather than throw it away, I stuck it in an arrangement of artificial flowers I had on our buffet table.

That was late summer several years ago.

I've since disposed of the feather but I'd kept it in the arrangement for quite some time.

To me, it served as a reminder of how close in harmony with nature we really are.

Even when we don't pursue it to meet a need in our own lives, a small creature such as a bird may see it as a way to meet a need in its own.

The cat that had wandered into our yard and stolen a bird from our sanctuary would perhaps come back again.

There is nothing to stop him.

And, after all, capturing an innocent bird is just a game to him. He's doing what for him comes naturally.

The bird, obviously, never suspected anything. He too was just doing what was natural for him—hunting and pecking for an insect or bug or feasting on the cracked corn or sunflower seeds I throw out for all the birds.

Experts call this the balance of nature.

I call it *death in my garden*.

Living in the country, I will have to get used to it.

In time, I suppose I will.

Section V

Biblical Reflections

Chapter 17

Mary and Joseph

"But you, Bethlehem Ephrathah, though you are small among the clans of Judah, out of you will come for me one who will be ruler over Israel, whose origins are from of old, from ancient times." (Micah 5:2, NIV)

E ach year as the Christmas story is told repeatedly in countless churches and auditoriums across our land, we're reminded of the sacrificial love that sent the Lord Jesus Christ to be born in humble circumstances to a peasant couple known only to God.

What was there about this couple that made them so different from those around them that God would single them out for so great a blessing? Was it their humility? Their love for God? Their obedience?

Scripture gives evidence to the fact that the young couple lived in humble circumstances. Luke 2:24 records that Mary's sacrifice for cleansing was "a pair of turtledoves or two young pigeons." Clearly, they could not afford a lamb for the offering.

But humility is not necessarily synonymous with poverty. Humility is rather a state of heart. Mary shows this humbleness of heart in her response to Elizabeth's greeting in Luke 1:45-46: *"...my soul exalts the Lord, and my spirit has rejoiced in God my Savior, for He has had regard for the humble state of His bondslave...."*

This same passage of Scripture (vv. 46-55) gives an indication of how much the Old Testament was known and loved in the home of Jesus. According to the Ryrie Study Bible, there are 15 discernible quotations from the Old Testament in this poem.

On speculation, human reasoning could conclude that God, in seeking a family for His Son, placed a great deal of importance on the fact that Jesus would be reared in a home filled with His knowledge and love.

One certainty is that Mary was but a young girl at the time of Jesus' birth. History records that Jewish girls married very young. Quite possibly, she was only 14 or 15.

One wonders if Mary, though willing, struggled with some of the same thoughts any girl her age would have wrestled with given the same circumstances: What will people think of me? How will I explain to Mother and Dad what has happened? Who will believe that I've spoken to an angel? Surely Joseph won't understand—what man would? What will become of me after this special baby is born? Will God take care of me?

And then there's Joseph. How was he different from other men? Was he stronger? More resolute in purpose? More able to bear up under pressure?

Quite evidently, Joseph was losing sleep over this puzzling dilemma he found himself in. He loved Mary dearly (after all, she was to be his bride!), but "being a man of stern principle," he knew he could no longer follow through with their wedding plans. He'd already decided he would break the engagement but wanted to do it quietly, as he didn't want to publicly disgrace her (Matthew 1:19).

However, when Joseph was told by his heavenly visitor in a dream (v. 20) that the child Mary would bear would be in fulfillment of a prophecy, he was no longer concerned about what action he should take as regards the Law. He obeyed without question. V.24-25 says, *"Then Joseph being raised from sleep did as the angel of the Lord had bidden him, and took unto him his wife:*

> *"And knew her not till she had brought forth her firstborn son: and he called his name JESUS."* (KJV)

Mary's obedience, as well, is recorded in Luke 1:38 (NKJV). When confronted with the news by the angel Gabriel that she would bear God's Son, her reply was, "Behold the maid-servant of the Lord! Let it be to me according to your word...."

Humility, a love for God, obedience. Yet despite these admirable qualities, even Mary and Joseph needed a Savior. "My soul exalts the Lord, and my spirit has rejoiced in God my Savior" is Mary's song in Luke 1:45-47. Although the blessed virgin Mary gave birth to the Savior of the world, she also recognized her own need for redemption.

Yes, the Christmas story is a love story. But, far more than the story of mere human love, it's rather the story of God's love as he sacrificially presented His Son to a lost and dying world.

Mary and Joseph were mere "avenues" of this love, but their devotion for both God and each other personifies this God-love for mankind. It's something we can relate to. And perhaps it's for this reason that the reenactment of this historical event continues to be of importance to both the believing, as well as to the unbelieving world.[26]

Chapter 18

Nehemiah

"Remember me with favor, my God." Nehemiah:
13:30 (NIV)

N ehemiah's return to Jerusalem in 444 BC to serve as governor was monumental. It had been 100 years since the return of the first Hebrew exiles under the decree of the Persian king, Cyrus, and the following decree by King Darius.

Few could have done it. But his character, as spelled out in the book after his name, shouts out the qualities of this man who, Scripture says, left his position as cupbearer to King Artaxerxes[27] and travelled to Jerusalem to orchestrate the rebuilding of the wall.

As in our present day, the Israelites were surrounded by the enemy. Without a wall to protect them, the thousands of Jews who now lived in the city proper were exposed and vulnerable, particularly in the darkness of night.

When one reads the account of Nehemiah, one has a tendency to zero in on (a) Nehemiah's prayer life—which, of course, was exemplary; also, (b) his tenacity in the actual rebuilding of the wall around Jerusalem.

But there are other insights to be gained as well. Here are several:

His sensitivity in spirit. In Chapter 1:2-3, when Hanani, Nehemiah's brother, comes to Susa where Nehemiah is serving King Artaxerxes as cupbearer and relates to Nehemiah the condition of Jerusalem, its gates and walls, and the disgrace its peoples are enduring, he, Nehemiah, reacts emotionally: *"When I heard these things, I sat down and wept" (Emphasis, mine. v.4).*

He entertained grief. *"For some days I mourned and fasted..."* Notice he didn't enter headlong into prayer but rather, prepared himself for it. So often, when we're overwhelmed with something that has taken us unawares or brings us great sorrow, we rush into prayer.

There are times when this is the most natural thing to do, but there are other times when we must search our hearts and minds *first*. We need to make sure there isn't anything that would block our prayers from being heard or answered.

King David did both. The years when he was on the run from King Saul and danger was often imminent, he prayed: *"Contend, LORD, with those who contend with me; fight against those who fight against me. Take up shield and armor; arise and come to my aid" (Psa. 35:1-2, NIV).*

He could do this because conversation with God was, for him, as natural as breathing.

The long, solitary nights he'd spent out on the Judean hillside shepherding his father's sheep had provided the opportunity to get to know God in a personal way. David actually welcomed the searchlight of God's Spirit on his soul. This brought him great peace. *"We wait in hope for the LORD; he is our help and our shield,"* echoed the words of his heart (Psa. 33:20).

Nehemiah obviously was searching his own heart as he mourned and fasted before praying aloud to God. His prayer is recorded in Chapter 1:5-10. He begins with praise:

> *"LORD, the God of heaven, the great and awe-some God, who keeps his covenant of love with those who love him and keep his command-ments, let your ear be attentive and your eyes open to hear the prayer your servant is praying before you day and night for your servants, the people of Israel" (vv. 5-6). (Emphasis, mine.)*

His prayer then naturally leads him into confession—for himself, his father's family and the Israelite nation as a whole:

"I confess the sins *we* Israelites, *including myself and my father's family*, have committed against you.

We have acted very wickedly toward you. *We* have not obeyed the commands, decrees and laws you gave your servant Moses." (vv. 6-7).

Nehemiah appeals to God in a way only someone who has maintained a personal relationship with God could.

First, he reminds God of the instruction he gave his servant Moses *'If you are unfaithful, I will scatter you among the nations….(*v. 8).

He goes on to remind God that, even if his exiled people were "at the farthest horizon," he would bring them back to that place especially chosen for his Name'" (v. 9).

And, of course, we know that chosen place to be Jerusalem.

It's interesting to note that many of us who were born prior to 1948 witnessed the formation of the State of Israel in our lifetime, although we might have been too young to understand what was happening at the time.

Many of us who are still living are witnessing this ongoing pilgrimage to the holy land today. God appears to be calling his people home. Daniel and several of the other prophets, including the Lord Jesus Himself, were emphatic about certain signs God's servants could watch for as the Day of the LORD grew nearer.

God continues to work out his time-table for Israel today and many evangelical preachers and teachers in particular regularly remind believers of these signs through their daily television and radio broadcasts.

A historic moment was when the United States, under the Republican leadership of President Donald J. Trump, brought Israel, the United Emeritus Republic, and Bahrain to the table to sign a trade agreement.

This took place in 2020. It had long been on the negotiating table.

An earlier historic moment (under the leadership of President Trump) was the Peace Accord Israel signed with Palestine.

Just prior to that, in 2019, the United States moved their embassy to Jerusalem.

Nehemiah also reminds God in his prayer on behalf of the Israelite nation that they are "his servants whom he redeemed by his great strength and [his] mighty hand."

Finally, Nehemiah closes his prayer (v. 11) by pleading with God to listen carefully to his servant and "to the prayer of [his] servants who delight in revering [His] name" and "that God might grant him favor in the presence of King Artaxerxes."

Reading through to the end of the book, we learn that Nehemiah's trust in Almighty God brought many blessings. And while it's true he had many trials to go through before he came to that place of blessing, the hope was always there.

Nehemiah's heart was fixed.

He had learned what it is to rely on God moment by moment, trusting him to be there for him through the bad as well as the good times. The people, while fearful themselves, were encouraged by the example Nehemiah set. His faith, obedience, reverence for God, and mindset gave them the motivation to work beyond what they felt their capabilities were and to stay with the task.

The end result was that the wall was rebuilt in 52 days! Can you not just imagine the sigh of relief expressed by these tired, dirty (they took little if any time for personal care), formerly disheartened people as they realized their work was done and the security for which they had greatly longed would now become a reality!

Nehemiah's strength came from his prayer life. Can we say the same thing? Perhaps not, but that should not prevent us from cultivating intimacy with God through time spent alone with him every day.

The psalmist David praised God every morning when he began his day. Should we do any less?

Chapter 19

Habakkuk

"For the earth will be filled with the knowledge
of the glory of the LORD as the waters cover
the sea." (Habakkuk 2:14, KJV²⁸)

H abakkuk was puzzled.
He wanted answers.
From God.

Answers to questions he'd been mulling over, perhaps for some time, as he observed Judah's leaders getting away with murder, as it were.

Scripture tells us, through Habakkuk, that the poor were being oppressed.

There was strife and conflict in the land.

The righteous were being exploited.

> *"Therefore the law is paralyzed,"* Habakkuk
> cries out to God, *"And justice never prevails."*
> (Hab.: 1-4, NIV, emphasis, added.)

Habakkuk knew to take his complaints to the LORD. He had a number of them and so, by grace, he enters into dialogue with the God of the universe: *"How long, LORD, must I call for help, but you do not listen? Or cry out to you, 'Violence!' but you do not save?"* (v. 2)

It's somewhat humorous to picture this lowly descendent of Adam's race addressing the Creator of all mankind with such boldness.

Where the fear?
Where the humility?
Where the knocking knees, the stuttering speech, the clammy hands?

Obviously, Habakkuk had entered into relationship with his Creator, the same kind Jesus' disciples had entered into with him while their Savior and Lord was still among them.

"I no longer call you servants," Jesus said in John 15:15, *"... instead, I have called you friends, for everything that I learned from my Father I have made known to you."*

God's love, and tolerance for, Habakkuk's insolence (if one could go so far as to suggest that) did not quell God's response to the prophet: *"Look at the nations and watch and be utterly amazed. For I am going to do something in your days that you would not believe, even if you were told."* (Hab. 1:5)

Habakkuk now is all ears. Obviously, he brought his concerns for his Israelite brothers before the LORD prior to this since we've already seen in v. 2 above where he pleads, *"How long, LORD, must I call for help, but you do not listen?"*

Have you ever talked to the Lord Jesus Christ about something, time and time again, and yet you see no evidence of answered prayer? As with David in the Psalms, you've searched your heart for anything that might be amiss.

And you've given God permission to do the same: *"Search me O God,"* is David's plea in Psa. 139:23-24 (NIV) *"and know my heart: test me and know my anxious thoughts. See if there is any offensive way in me, and lead me in the way everlasting."* (Emphasis, added.)

I've heard TV evangelists suggest reasons why God does not answer earnest prayer:

There's sin in our lives.
There's someone we need to forgive.
Our spiritual life is not in order.
We're not taking time, daily, to come before the Lord..

And while all these things do enter into unanswered prayer, there are, nevertheless, certain things God simply chooses not to share with us. Deuteronomy 29:29 (CSB) says, *"The hidden things belong to the LORD our God, but the revealed things belong to us and our children forever…"*

In my own prayer life, I've discovered that God has his will and his ways. His timing for answered prayer is not necessarily my timing. I've shared in my book, *"Heaven's Scent: Spreading the Fragrance of Christ"*[29] where a close member of our family had, after much prayer and persuasion on our part, yielded up his life to Christ at a Billy Graham Crusade.

It had been a number of years since we, Russ and I, had begun praying for Evan's[30] salvation, and every witnessing encounter had brought only more conviction and, on one occasion, anger on his part.

We prayed God would cut through his anger, cut through his pride, and cut through his seeming inability to bend to the authority of Christ. We also prayed God would put down the enemy of his soul, Satan.

While it's too much to go into here, the point I want to make is that, finally, at a particular Evangelistic Crusade in Seattle, through the work of the Holy Spirit and the encouragement of our friends, Evan prayed to invite Jesus Christ into his life.

"Thank you, Jesus," I prayed silently as, with a thankful heart, I thanked the God of the Universe who never gives up on us.

Admittedly, there were times after that when, perhaps because of his age (68), I wondered if the commitment Evan made that night was real. But on his deathbed, I was given that assurance.

In Habakkuk's dialogue with God, we've already seen where God responded by telling Habakkuk that he, God, was going *to do something in [his] days that [he] would not believe, even if [he] were told."*

Now God, in his graciousness toward his servant, Habakkuk, shares with him his plan:

"I am raising up the Babylonians," God says in Hab. 1:6, *"that ruthless and impetuous people, who sweep across the whole earth to seize dwellings not their own."*

Then, in continuing dialogue with Habakkuk, God, in poetic prose, goes on to describe what the Babylonian army is like and how ruthless they are when they go into battle.

Stay with me, dear Reader, as we read the account from the Scriptures. Together, we will get caught up emotionally with the sound of the galloping horses and the battle cry of the warriors as their cavalry charges through the nations, sweeping across the entire then-known earth, "[advancing] like a desert wind and gathering prisoners like sand." (v. 9)

> *"They are a feared and dreaded people;*
> *They are a law to themselves*
> *And promote their own honor.*
> *Their horses are swifter than leopards,*
> *Fiercer than wolves at dusk.*
> *Their cavalry gallops headlong;*
> *Their horsemen come from afar.*
> *They fly like an eagle swooping to devour;*
> *They all come intent on violence.*
> *Their hordes advance like a desert wind*
> *And gather prisoners like sand.*
> *They mock kings*
> *And scoff at rulers.*
> *They laugh at all fortified cities;*
> *By building earthen ramps they capture them.*
> *Then they sweep past like the wind and go on—*
> *Guilty people, whose own strength is their god."*
> *Habakkuk 1:5-11 (NIV, emphasis, added).*

Habakkuk ends his dialog with God with a beautiful prayer of faith which Christians have memorized and relied on for centuries.

> *Though the fig tree does not bud*
> *And there are no grapes on the vines,*
> *Though the olive crop fails*
> *And the fields produce no food,*
> *Though there are no sheep in the pen*

And no cattle in the stalls,
Yet I will rejoice in the LORD,
I will be joyful in God my Savior.
Habakkuk 3:17-18 (NIV).

I'm often moved to tears when, in reading the Voice of the Martyrs' monthly magazine to supporters[31], I'm reminded of how Christians in other parts of the world are suffering indescribably for their faith.

Some to the point of martyrdom.

President Cole Richards, in the October 2021 issue of the VOM, poses a rhetorical question to his readers: "But how can we show love toward those who insult and abuse us? Our persecuted Christian family members have this to teach us: The most important way we can show love to our enemies is by sharing the truth of Christ with them."

Many of us perhaps will never enter into a close relationship with someone who belongs to a faith that makes it a crime to practice Christianity, but we can pray for them.

We can pray that God will enlighten them to what it means to be a Christian.

And we can pray that God would give them the courage to live out their lives for him. Many converts to Christianity still fear physical harm, even though they are now living in a country known for its tolerance to other faiths.

We can seek to understand, through listening and learning, what warms the heart of an individual whose heart he left behind in his own country, while his head is trying to absorb the unfamiliar ways of his adoptive country.

Years ago, when Russ accepted a position as a manufacturing engineer with VERTOL[32] in Philadelphia, we knew it would mean, eventually, our embracing citizenship in the United States.

This, in a sense, meant turning our back on Canada, which we didn't want to do.

To be honest, the decision was made with our heads. It would take much longer for the transaction to take place in our hearts. So, to a point, I understand how difficult it must be for immigrants and refugees to leave behind everything familiar to them; i.e., all their possessions, job titles (security), family and friends.

Prayer with and for these people is needed to make them feel accepted in their new country.

Are those of us who name the name of Christ up to putting feet to the gospel message of Jesus Christ and opening our hearts and homes to them?

Perhaps not. It's a big order.

But, can we at least pray that God will help us support those who will?

Prayer: Lord, please give each of us the resources that will allow us to meet not only our own needs but also the needs of those who have come to us empty-handed seeking refuge in our country. Amen.

Chapter 20

Daniel

"My heart is set on keeping your decrees to the very end." Psalm 119:11[2]

The kingdom was in an uproar. King Nebuchadnezzar was having a royal tantrum. He'd had a nightmare to end all nightmares and he wanted one of his wise men; i.e., magicians, enchanters, sorcerers, astrologers, to interpret his dream for him.

Their response, *"Tell your servants the dream, and we will interpret it."*

This was not to the king's liking.

King Nebuchadnezzar had already decided if they could not recount his dream to him, he would *"have [you] cut into pieces and your houses turned into piles of rubble."* (Read the entire account in Daniel 2.)

One can only imagine the terror these mortals experienced in their hearts. They tried again: "Let the king tell his servants the dream, and we will interpret it."

Certain that they were stalling for time, the king counters with, "You have conspired to tell me misleading and wicked things, hoping the situation will change. *So then, tell me the dream, and I will know that you can interpret it for me."* (Emphasis, added.)

By now, surely the magicians, enchanters, sorcerers, and astrologers were trembling in their sandals, throwing up their hands in dismay, tearing their robes, and perhaps, as we might say, sweating buckets.

The astrologers dared to speak up in their defense: "What the king asks is too difficult. No one can reveal it to the king except the gods...."

King Nebuchadnezzar flew into a rage. His head thrown back, the veins in his neck taut and protruding, his face red as a vine-ripened tomato in summer, his eyes bulging from their sockets, his teeth clenched, his whole body stiff and unyielding, his fists tightened in knots at his sides, he proceeded to roar the order to have all the wise men in the kingdom executed.

This decree, of course, was to include Daniel and his friends, Hananiah, Mishael and Azariah. (Read about these three faithful Jewish men in chapter 3.)

When Daniel got the word, rather than bemoan his probable fate and the fate of his three friends, he remained calm and took steps to look into the matter.

First, he enquired of Arioch, the commander of the king's guard: *"Why did the king issue such a harsh decree?"*

When apprised of the reason for it, rather than give in to his fears—if indeed he had any—he went directly to the source— the king himself. The king, surprisingly, granted Daniel an audience, agreeing to give Daniel time *"so that he might inter-pret the dream for him."*

The king by this time had obviously gotten control of his rage, else he wouldn't have granted Daniel this tête-à-tête. He also evidently remembered the initial interview he'd held with Daniel and his three friends shortly after they were brought to Babylon as Israelite captives (Read the whole account in Daniel, Chapter 1).

In that particular interview (v.17), Scripture says, *"To these four young men God gave knowledge and understanding of all kinds of literature and learning. And Daniel could understand visions and dreams of all kinds." (*Emphasis, mine.)

Second, Daniel shared the matter with Hananiah, Mishael and Azariah, asking them to pray for God's mercy so that their lives would be spared. God heard and answered their prayers.

Worthy of note here is the prayer of *praise* and *thanksgiving* Daniel prayed that night, for God revealed to him, in a vision, both the dream and the interpretation of the dream:

> *"Praise be to the name of God*
> *for ever and ever;*
> *wisdom and power are his.*
> *He changes times and*
> *seasons;*
> *he deposes kings and raises*
> *up others.*
> *He gives wisdom to the wise*
> *and knowledge to the*
> *discerning.*
> *He reveals deep and hidden*
> *things;*
> *he knows what lies in*
> *darkness,*
> *and light dwells with him.*
> *I thank and praise you, God of*

my ancestors:
You have given me wisdom
and power,
you have made known to me
what we asked of you,
you have made known to us
The dream of the king." (Dan. 1:20-23, NIV)

Third, Daniel goes back to Arioch and requests he not carry out the king's orders as issued, but rather take him (Daniel) to the king. "I will interpret his dream for him," he says in Chapter 2:24.

Obviously, Daniel, over time, has gained the confidence of the king's guard and can make this request and know that it is within his right to do so.

Fourth, Daniel wisely explains to the king, when asked, if he, Daniel, could interpret the dream and tell him what it meant. Daniel's response—*No wise man, enchanter, magician or diviner can explain to the king the mystery he has asked about*—[33]is intended to set the record straight and to perhaps prevent a like event from happening in the future.

He, Daniel, then goes on to say, *"but there is a God in heaven who reveals mysteries. He has shown King Nebuchadnezzar what will happen in days to come" (v.28).*

One can only imagine the intensity with which the king listens as Daniel describes Nebuchadnezzar's dream, as well as its interpretation. (See Dan. 1:28-45.)

When he is finished, Daniel tells King Nebuchadnezzar that God has shown him what will take place in the future (v.45). And lest the king would have any doubts about the veracity of either the explanation or the interpretation of the dream, he states emphatically, *"The dream is true and its interpretation is trustworthy."*

Finally, King Nebuchadnezzar, aside from his explosive temper, does make good on his promise to honor the wise man who could interpret his dream. (See Dan. 1:6, 2:46-49.) Additionally, he honors Daniel's request to have his three friends, Hananiah, Mishael and Azariah elevated to higher positions within the Babylonian kingdom.

In this particular instance, one might conclude, "All is well that ends well."

ଔଔଔଔଔଔଔ

Take away from Daniel:

Scripture doesn't tell us how old Daniel and his three friends were when taken to Babylon as captives in 605 BC. One would assume, based on Chapter 1, they were still teenagers and so considered pliable, teachable and, after training, qualified to serve in the palace of King Nebuchadnezzar.

Daniel was obviously set apart by God and to God for a special purpose. His ability to interpret dreams and to *see* into the future were unique gifts that were given to him to be used, not only for that time, but for a future time as well:

> *"The vision of the evenings and mornings that has been given you is true, but seal up the vision, for it concerns the distant future" (Dan. 8:26, NIV, Emphasis added).*

Daniel is further instructed by *"the man clothed in linen," (v. 7) to "go [his] way because the words are rolled up and sealed until the time of the end" (v. 9).*

Many Christ-followers today, in reading the Scriptures, tend to stick to the New Testament, almost to the exclusion of the Old Testament. Perhaps they find the NT easier to read or they've been taught the OT is not for our times. But, when you consider the wealth of information contained in the History books, the Prophetic books, to say nothing of the Psalms (Songs) of King David, the Wisdom books of King Solomon, and others, you have to wonder if they are not cheating themselves.

Worse still, are they not doing God a disfavor?

Section Vi

New Year's Resolutions

Chapter 21

Getting Spiritually Fit

> *"All Scripture is God-breathed and is useful for teaching, rebuking, correcting and training in righteousness, so that the servant of God may be thoroughly equipped for every good work."*
> 2 Timothy 3:16 (NIV)

A recent fitness advertisement stated, *"If over 90% of people know they should be more active, why are so few actually exercising on a regular basis?"*

This same question could be asked in the spiritual realm: *Why aren't more Christ-followers disciplined in the area of Bible study, spending time alone with God in prayer, and in attending church regularly?*

As with fitness, some slackness in these areas stems out of laziness. Some is in holding the wrong priorities. Still some is simply lack of motivation or concern.

The advertisement goes on to say, *"Many people have the wrong idea about exercise…These people don't understand that increased activity can and should be a natural, enjoyable part of everyday life—not some grim and punishing experience."*

And so it is with the spiritual. A daily, consistent walk with the Lord should not be a forced thing but rather an enjoyable part of every day life.

If you, like me, can identify with the masses when it comes to setting into place and maintaining spiritual disciplines—particularly when it comes to Bible study—you might want to consider the following:

1. ***Easing yourself into shape***. Develop a specific plan. Read a secular book on time management. Learn from the experts. Don't leave Bible disciplines to chance. If you do, you're apt to get busy with something else and your good intentions will evaporate like an early morning mist. Or, you'll be too tired. Then you'll convince yourself there's *always another day.*

2. ***Setting realistic goals***. Many people get turned off on Bible study because they attempt to read the Bible through in a fixed length of time, say a year. This is a fine goal for seasoned readers, but if you're just getting attuned to the need to be in the Word, don't take on Mount Everest. Ask your pastor or Christian Ed person to give you guidance here. There are many good Bible study plans available to both the serious student and the daily dipper. Ask them to recommend one.

3. ***Using motivational equipment***. Whether your desire is to become a serious student of the Word or someone who simply wants to walk in obedience to the Lord

(and, really, do we have a choice?), you will need some tools to motivate you. Commentaries, handbooks, and study guides are invaluable as are Christian periodicals that stress doctrine and/or life application. Again, check with your Christian Education committee for ideas. While these books can be and often are expensive, your church library may be a good resource. If your church no longer maintains a library, then turn to the World Wide Web—a constant resource which has 24-hour access.

4. ***Establishing a definite time and place.*** Make an appointment with God. Chances are, if you do, you will make it a habit. Use that cell phone or little black book you carry around in your sports jacket or pocketbook and mark off (in color for emphasis!) time to meet with God daily. *And stick to it!*

5. ***Involving your family and friends.*** Recently, a single parent and several other singles from our church established a Bible reading time after the Sunday evening service. It's a small group, but they are an encouragement to one another and, in time, could prove to be a motivational force within the church. Involve your family in your Bible reading time, too. It may soon become a custom you will all enjoy and one that has lasting benefits.

6. ***Varying your activity.*** Even as bodily exercise can quickly become *old hat*, so can Bible study if you don't vary your approach to it. This is one good reason to use

a study guide. Various Christian ministry organizations are continually coming up with interesting and exciting ways to read and study God's Word and they are eager to pass them along to us, generally for a nominal fee. Keep a pencil or pen handy and note the web address or phone number to call when they air over the radio, TV or your cell phone.

7. **Keeping track of your progress.** On-again, off-again habit patterns are often recognized and can more easily be overcome if you chart your progress. Many of us enjoy keeping charts for exercise, diet control, and a host of other things. The use of this same method is still another positive way to encourage self-motivation in Bible study. It's always encouraging to look back over several days, months, and years and discover that you've made real headway.

Finally, expect to be rewarded. Every positive endeavor produces fruit, and time spent alone with God is no exception. *"Call to me,"* says the Lord through the prophet Jeremiah, *"and I will answer you and tell you great and unsearchable things you do not know."*[34]

Spiritual exercise, like bodily exercise, should become part of the growing Christian's lifestyle. Making it work for you and me takes time and effort but the rewards are well worth it.

Chapter 22

Resolution to Change

"Resolutions to diet, exercise, or meet a certain goal seldom come to fruition. The human flesh is just too weak and undisciplined." (Author unknown.)

Several years ago, I decided to try a new approach to New Year's resolutions. I broke them down into three categories:

- Physical

- Spiritual

- Mental

The physical was in the area of exercise. For this, I joined *Curves*. My health insurance company paid for it and I could go as often as I wanted to, *gratis*!

I also had in mind that I wanted to use this opportunity to share Christ with others. This did not work as most of the women came with friends and left with those same friends. They did not need to respond to my overtures for friendship.

More recently, before I married Jay and moved to Georgia, I joined a line-dancing class at the Lebanon Senior Center near where I lived. I went alone, vowing to reach out and meet other women who, like myself, were aging and knew they needed *to do something* to stay limber.

This group of ladies was different! I met four or five women who, like me, wanted to make friends as well as reach their exercising goals.

There was one lady there, in particular, who, while in her 91st year, had more get up and go than many of us who were much younger!

I went on several day bus trips with these ladies and enjoyed my time with them thoroughly. Women who live alone can indeed have a lot of fun together when they make up their mind to!

This all ended just before I married Jay. By now my focus had changed and my time and efforts were spent on making wedding preparations. But I will always remember these special ladies and their friendliness toward me and acceptance of me and my opportunity to speak up on Christ's behalf.

ଉଚ୍ଚଉଚ୍ଚଉଚ୍ଚଉଚ୍ଚ

In the spiritual realm, my personal goals were simple: I wanted to discover new things in the Bible I hadn't seen before. I decided to do this by reading several newer translations and using the King James Version for backup study only.

I also wanted to spend more time in *quality* prayer. I did this by purchasing a notebook and dividing it into sections:

1. Family, listing each one by name.

2. Siblings, again listing them by name as well as their needs as I became apprised of them.

3. Church; i.e., the leadership; the ladies' Sunday school class, in particular, as I was leading the class at the time; my closest friends, and so on.

I divided my time in segments: So much time for reading the Old Testament, so much time for the New Testament—so much time for prayer and, finally, so much time for reading a current book written by one of the many well-known Christian authors who are popular today.

All this took me about an hour and a half to two hours daily, excluding Sundays, and the time went quickly!

I was able to stick to this challenge by getting up very early in the morning and treating myself to a cup of hot herbal tea, a cup of yogurt or nuts or crackers and cheese or a breakfast bar. This tasty nourishment made my appointment with the Lord more enjoyable *and* more beneficial as it helped me to concentrate better. I wasn't thinking about my tummy!

Some mornings, of course, I gave in to the flesh and stayed in bed rather than get up to read or study. But, most mornings, over time, I did realize considerable success. (I have maintained this regimen over the years. The only time I had to change my schedule was the eleven years I worked after Michael and Diana started college. I had to switch to just before I went to bed. That did work but I had to shorten my time with the Lord as I got sleepy.)

Incidentally, there is wisdom in coming before the Lord first thing in the *morning*. In Psa. 92:1-2, the psalmist says, "It is good to praise the LORD and make music to your name, O Most High, proclaiming your love *in the morning.....*" (Italics, mine). *Why*? For one reason, it sets the tone for the day. It's hard to be grumpy or short-tempered when you've just enjoyed sweet fellowship with the Lord.

For another thing, our minds are clearer. Most times we are rested and I do believe the Lord honors our efforts by giving us a clearer vision of His will for our lives, day by day. Or He may lay upon our heart someone for whom He would have us to pray. Or he may bring to mind promises and certain passages of Scripture that He would have us to look at more closely.

ಐಐಐಐಐಐಐ

The third category I marked off in my New Year's Resolutions notebook was "*mental*."

By mental, I mean something that would challenge me to think more deeply, not that God's Word didn't, but something that would force me to take a greater interest in the world around me.

Before the general election at that time, I watched many of the newscasts on several of the news channels to try to prepare myself to vote knowledgeably and intelligently.

I listened with an open mind to these broadcasts and tried to catch most of the interviews when candidates were being interviewed by the press.

I don't believe God ever intended that Christians hide their heads in the sand when it comes to world events. I actually learned this from my late husband, Russ. While not an avid reader, he did take a vital interest in the news, both local and nationally, and could hold his own with the best of them when controversial issues sprung up in conversation.

So much of the news is commentary and, as I see it, of little use overall. But the catastrophes, world events and political happenings should be of interest and of value to the Christian, in particular, if he/she wants to pray knowledgeably about, not only our own country, but other countries of the world as well.

The Bible says that, *"In the same way that iron sharpens iron, a person sharpens the character of his friend."* (Prov. 27:17 *The Voice*, Ecclesia Bible Society, Thomas Nelson.)

Russ often said he learned more from listening to others than he did from reading. Everyone, of course, has his own way of gathering facts. Whatever works for you, then that's the way to do it!

CRCRCRCRCRCRCRCR

Finally, to sum up my thoughts on the subject of making New Year's Resolutions, I would say that it's important to reassess our thinking from time to time—to challenge ourselves to think circumspectly about how and what we are doing with the years the Lord has given us on this earth. Are we investing our time wisely or are we wasting it?

With eternity in view and the time drawing near for Christ's return[35], we need to make any changes that are necessary to bring ourselves, with his help, to a state of maturity.

I'm reminded of the apostle Paul's words in Philippians 3:13,14: *"But one thing I do: Forgetting what is behind and straining toward what is ahead, I press on toward the goal to win the prize for which God has called me heavenward in Christ Jesus"* (NIV, italics, mine.)

Every time I read and meditate on this verse, I can envisage once again our daughter Diana running her heart out at a local or state track meet—a champion in so many ways and, like her competitors, sprinting to cross the finish line—even if it killed her.

The few seconds that it took to strain for that last big push meant winning or losing, not just the race of the moment, but for the school's athletic reputation for the whole year, and sometimes beyond that.

It was the culmination of hours and hours of practice, running up and down bleachers and to and from class, learning not to complain when you're tired, and enduring long tiresome days on the bus to and from track meets.

Was it exhilarating? Of course. Putting your whole heart and soul into anything is exhilarating.

Paul knew that. He chose his illustration well. He wanted Christ's followers to understand that their lot would not be an easy one. There would be no letting up. They would have to cross that finish line. But, once they did, there would be a reward waiting for them that would be far superior to any award a sprinter would receive at a track meet.

It would be to hear God's call to resurrection life found exclusively in Jesus the Anointed.[36]

Chapter 23

Bible Reading Discipline

Oh, how I love your law! I meditate on it all day long. Your commands are always with me and make me wiser than my enemies. (Psalm 119:97-98, NIV.)

I t was a great day for a walk. The air was brisk and cool, the sun was shining overhead. "Let's go for a walk," I said. "Sure," was my husband's response.

Russ and I often went for walks in and through our neighborhood. About three to four times a week, actually. We loved the slight breeze that blew in our faces as we walked along and the pull of our leg muscles as we increased our stride.

Walking, or exercise of any kind, is sometimes difficult work in the beginning. Just getting your coat on and getting out the door is a struggle for some. But when exercise becomes a habit, it's amazing how much satisfaction you derive from it.

Bible reading is not a great deal unlike physical exercise. You want to do it, you set aside time to do it, but so many other things, good things, come up to keep you from it. Things like making a phone call to a friend, getting cards ready for the mail, or taking your grandson for a ride.

But God says reading his word, and digesting it is like eating honey. Although some aspects of it, like exercise, may be bitter to take, overall it is sweet to the soul. Psalm 119:103-104 (NIV) says this: "How sweet are your words to my taste, sweeter than honey to my mouth! I gain understanding from your precepts; therefore I hate every wrong path".

For me, reading the Bible is a way of life. I seldom let a day go by without opening its pages and pouring over the truths in Scripture. Many people, unfortunately, don't read the Bible because they're afraid God will ask them to do something they're unprepared to do: call a friend and ask forgiveness for an offense, tell someone about Jesus, or visit a sick neighbor. And it's true that sometimes God does ask us to do difficult things. But, if and when he does, he always gives us the strength to do it.

I recall one incident in particular when I was new to Bible study and prayer. I wanted to heed God's command to walk in obedience to him. But I felt he wanted me to make overtures to the woman next door, a woman whose friendship I shied away from because of my own feelings of inadequacy. Only later, this same woman, Florence, offered to help me wallpaper a bedroom. I agreed and thanked her for desire to help. But when the time came, I made sure I'd begun much earlier than I had told her I would. I was afraid Florence would take over and the project would become hers rather than mine.

Florence, after assessing the situation, said: "Well, if I'm not needed here, I'll go home..."

She had stayed only one hour.

I knew Florence had been slighted by my thoughtlessness, and I was genuinely sorry. I also knew that, ultimately, I would have to go to her and apologize. I couldn't continue to open God's Word and to pray until I was ready to obey his commands. So, early one evening, shortly after dark, I prayed to the Holy Spirit for courage and started out across our property lines.

My feet felt like lead and my heart melted within me at the prospects of actually knocking on my neighbor's door. But after I'd gone the first few steps, something strange happened. Suddenly my feet grew lighter and my legs just seemed to carry me along. It was almost as if *Someone* else were walking in my shoes. At once, I found myself at her door.

Timidly, I knocked and waited. "Yes?" Florence queried, peering out from behind the door curtain. Then, seeing it was me, she opened the door. Her look of consternation soon turned into a smile. I relaxed and, at her invitation, entered her home. "Thank you, Lord," I breathed silently.

As I explained my mission, Florence listened quietly. Then, once again, she offered to help me with yet another project—this time it would be preparing flower beds.

God's Word contains many commands and promises. But unless I read His Word, I will never know what these are and will never be able to apply them to my life and to my situation.

Like exercise, it's important that I establish a regular time to meet with God—an appointment, if you will.

Then I need to make sure I keep that appointment.

The joy that comes from obeying his commands is *my present* reward and any reward that Christ deems worthy will be given to me (*and to you!*) at his Second Coming (I Thess. 5:13-17, NIV).

Section Vii

Letter Writing

Chapter 24

A Note to Writers

"This is the covenant I will make with the people of Israel after that time," declares the LORD, I will put my law in their minds and write it on their hearts. I will be their God, and they will be my people...." (Jeremiah 31:33, NIV.)

When Jesus Christ in Matthew 28:19-20 instructed the early church to "go and make disciples of all nations...." He gave them the motivation for doing so.

He would return for them.[37]

They would receive rewards for their labor.[38]

They would be given a new name, known only to them.[39]

They would be acknowledged before the Father and his angels.[40]

They would reign with him.[41]

With the motivation came the power or authority to carry out his will. This would be coupled with the sense of urgency: "Therefore keep watch, because you do not know on what day your Lord will come" (Matt. 24:42, NIV).

As writers whose desire it is to bring others to Jesus Christ and to disciple them, we too must hold to these same principles.

First, we motivate our readers by pointing them to the Savior. This is done by skillfully weaving God's Word into the text of our writing. It is God's Word, coupled with the power and influence of God's Spirit, that brings conviction, not ours. This means that we ourselves must stay close to Him.

Second, we must motivate our readers to move beyond a mere emotional response to God's Word to a response that will bring about permanent change in their lives, a move that will take them beyond apathy to the producing of genuine fruit in their lives.

Third, we need to motivate them to consider the urgency of the hour. Even as Jesus instructed his disciples, in so many words, to keep focused, we too must somehow convey to our readers the importance of putting spiritual matters ahead of the acquisition of wealth, the right to personal happiness and the right to do it my way.

It's a challenge, certainly.

But it's a challenge we as writers must undertake if we are to become those who would disciple our nation for Christ. And the challenge becomes a joy if we remember Who it is we are serving and why we are doing it.

Chapter 25

A Forgotten Ministry

"He has made us competent as ministers of a
new covenant—not of the letter but of the Spirit;
for the letter kills, but the Spirit gives life." 2
Corinthians 3:6, NIV

On a particular Saturday some years ago, I received a surprise letter from a friend. "At the risk of causing a mild coronary," she wrote, "I decided to drop you a short note....."

This particular friend had extremely poor eyesight, and I knew it was a hardship for her to write several pages of greeting. But she did it because she knew it would mean a lot to me.

In the days of the early church, letter writing was a ministry. The apostle Paul, for instance, used letter writing often and well. In his correspondence to the young churches, his letters were weighty. They were written to instruct, to teach, to bring encouragement. And they are still doing that today.

I, too, have discovered letter writing can be a ministry—a way to give of myself, my time, my talent to God's service. The rewards are measured not only in terms of enjoyment, but in the knowledge that I'm using still another avenue available to me with which to win the unreached for Jesus Christ.

After we had moved away from Pennsylvania, for instance, Russ was told that it was through a letter written to a particular pastor some years ago and a visit prompted by that letter that God used to bring his wife Lily to Christ.

Lily had been dying from cancer. According to her doctors, she had less than six months to live. I was concerned. Would anyone share Jesus with her?

My family and I were living several thousand miles away when we heard of Lily's illness. How could we reach Lily for Jesus Christ?

I prayed, asking God to show me a way. God brought to mind a young woman I'd met in the hospital when our son Michael was born. Charie had shared her father's testimony with me. I didn't understand the spiritual implication of it then. It had been simply an interesting story.

But several years and a long-distance move later, both Russ and I came to faith in Christ. Now, in praying for Lily, I remembered the testimony.

I also remembered The Blue Church in Pennsylvania that had been recommended as having a Bible-based outreach. We had driven past that particular church many times and commented on its uniqueness, particularly in its name. I knew this church was situated within a few blocks of where Lily and John lived.

I didn't know who pastored the church. I didn't have its full street address or official name. But I took a chance on writing anyway. I had to. My friend's soul was at stake.

Several years later, mutual friends were visiting in the Pacific Northwest. Vi and Orville told us about Lily's death and funeral.

"It was strange," they said, "Lily had a traditional church background, but it was the pastor from The Blue Church who buried her."

Strange? Not really. Letters have a way of starting chain reactions. Members of my own family have been ministered to in a similar way.

Because letter writing is a ministry for me, I wince when I hear people say, "But I don't have time to write letters!" Inwardly I think, but neither did Paul, and his letters to the churches comprise most of the New Testament.

I'm glad he took the time.

Epilogue

Jesus said…"I am the resurrection and the life. The one who believes in me will live, even though they die; and whoever lives by believing in me will never die." John 11:25-26 (NIV)

It was a call we were not looking forward to but a call we had been expecting for several weeks. "John has passed," Sarah said. "He died at 3 o'clock."

Jay quickly expressed his sympathy and turned up the speaker on the phone. He knew I would want to hear what Sarah had to say about the plans they, the family, and she had made for John's funeral.

"We're only having family there," Sarah said, repeating what she had already expressed to us in a prior call a few days' earlier. "It will be at the church. We didn't want to be responsible for anyone being exposed to COVID. We thought it best to keep it small."

Sarah then went on to say that a book would be in the Vestibule of the church if anyone wanted to stop by and sign it.

Jay thanked Sarah for calling us. He and John had known each other for most of their lives. Sarah, too, had been a friend of the family very early on and often spoke of Jay's mother, Eunice.

"We all loved her as a Sunday school teacher," Sarah said on several occasions when she was sharing with me some of her memories of the family.

And while Jay had been away from his home town for thirty years and their paths took them in different directions, he and John were always glad to see each other at church and other familiar places when Jay returned to the area.

Attending John's funeral would have given Jay that opportunity to say his final *goodbye* but he understood the family's wishes and he respected their concern for others in making their decision.

As a Christian, he knew that he would see John again some day. Perhaps they would pick up where they left off in conversation and John would share with Jay his memory of a particular fishing or hunting expedition.

For the Christian, death is never final. It's merely an open door to what is waiting for them on the *Other Side*.

Thankfully, death is no longer kept in the back side of the parlor any more. People are no longer expected to wear black at a funeral, although some still do.

Lay persons are given the nod to conduct the final service when a favorite pastor is no longer in the area or perhaps is himself deceased.

Music tapes are offered or one's favorite pianist is given the go-ahead to set the tone for the funeral service. More often than not, a favorite niece or nephew, mid-way through the service, will read a poem they've written about the loved one, or sing a song he or she had loved, or tell an interesting, or sometimes humorous, anecdote they often shared.

Funeral homes are used more often than not for both the viewing *and* service because they are larger than many of the local churches. They can accommodate more people. They are designed with sitting rooms and restrooms that are well-lighted and situated, in most instances, just off the vestibule for convenience's sake.

Trained staff are on hand to lead a family member or guest to where they should wait for the service to begin. All is well planned and orchestrated to make the final moments of the deceased a pleasant memory for their loved ones.

Hearses, too, have not been left out in the overall attempt to make saying *goodbye* to a friend or loved one more palatable. Rather than the all-black Cadillac or Chrysler with drawn curtains, they may be white, navy blue or silver. Again, every attempt is now being made to give the loved one a proper sendoff and to ease the emotional pain of those left behind.

And it doesn't start there. When my beloved husband, Russ, expired at home and the hospice nurse called the undertaker to pick up his body, one of his men came to the front door fully dressed in a tuxedo and white gloves! It was near midnight! Most of our neighbors would have been asleep.

Not knowing their protocol, I suggested they remove his remains through the back door and out through the garage. His hospice nurse had made up his bed in the family room and this would have made it easier for them, rather than inching their way with the guerney through the hallway, out through the front door, and down the steps to where the hearse waited in the drive.

But they kindly indicated they would prefer to use the front door.

You know, I really appreciated that, after I had time to think about it. That particular funeral company had a high-end volume of business and I could certainly understand why.

Additionally, they offered every service needed, not only for the viewing, but for the aftermath of the funeral itself: a grief class, information on the purchase of headstones, where flowers could be purchased by visitors, and other suggestions I no longer recall or, in all probability, availed myself of. After all, we had the church body to look to for support and I knew to call on the pastor and/or deacons if I had a need.

My family did not live nearby so there would be those occasions when I would have to call on either the church or a neighbor for support. These occasions would be few and far between, but they did happen several times. Thankfully, those whom I called on were available and assured me they were glad they could be of help.

Michael, too, came down on several occasions to lend a helping hand.

Sarah's circumstances are different so she will, perhaps, give up her home and go directly into a residence facility. This will ease not only her concerns about preparing meals and keeping up her house and grounds, as well as maintaining her car, but she will not be alone at night. The latter is a fear that, for some women, never goes away. Some may be able to work their way through it while others may not.

Suffice is to say that death is never a welcome visitor. But it's something all of us must face and the more information we have about it, the better.

If someone were to ask me where they should look to find this information, I would first direct them to the Scriptures. The most important thing any of us can do in this life is prepare for death. Perhaps that sounds morbid but when you consider our lives here on earth are for but a moment in time whereas eternity is forever, it behooves us to make sure we're ready when we get the call.

Some reading this may not believe in the hereafter. And, of course, that's their right. Certainly, many don't. But for those who do, having a firm grip on what the Bible teaches about the afterlife brings a source of comfort to both the one whose life is fading, as well as for the one who weeps at their bedside saying their goodbyes.

There are a number of passages in both the Old and New Testaments that point to the *sleep of death* of the Christian believer. Paul, for instance, in I Thessalonians 4:13-17 encourages the believers in Thessalonica this way:

> *Brothers and sisters, we do not want you to be uninformed about those who sleep in death, so that you do not grieve like the rest of mankind, who have no hope. For we believe that Jesus died and rose again, and so we believe that God will bring with Jesus those who have fallen asleep in him. According to the Lord's word, we tell you that we who are still alive, who are left until the coming of the Lord, will certainly not precede those who have fallen asleep. For the Lord himself will come down from heaven, with a loud command, with the voice of the archangel and with the trumpet call of God, and the dead in Christ will rise first. After that, we who are still alive and are left will be caught up together with them in the clouds to meet the*

Lord in the air. And so we will be with the Lord
forever. Therefore encourage one another with
these words. (Emphasis, added.)

And Jesus himself, in endeavoring to comfort his disciples
prior to his death by crucifixion, says this in John 14:1-3:

"Do not let your hearts be troubled. You believe
in God; believe also in me. My Father's house
has many rooms; if that were not so, would I
have told you that I am going there to prepare
a place for you? And if I go and prepare a place
for you, I will come back and take you to be with
me that you also may be where I am."

Jesus' resurrection proves that what He said will come to
pass. Even as death and the grave could not hold him, neither
will it be able to hold those of us who are believers.

This is not to say our bodies will not decay over time, but
in God's timing, at Christ's command, our bodies will be res-
urrected and we will be reunited with our loved ones.[42]

And while there is much about heaven that we do not
understand, we can catch a glimpse of it afar off in the book
of Revelation. For example, in Revelation 21:22-26, John
describes heaven like this:

I [John] did not see a temple in the city
[Jerusalem], because the Lord God Almighty
and the Lamb are its temple. The city does not
need the sun or the moon to shine on it, for
the glory of God gives it light, and the Lamb

[Jesus] is its lamp. The nations will walk by its light, and the kings of the earth will bring their splendor into it. On no day will its gates ever be shut, for there will be no night there. The glory and honor of the nations will be brought into it. Nothing impure will ever enter it, nor will anyone who does what is shameful or deceitful, but only those whose names are written in the Lamb's book of life.

If you who are reading this desire to trust Christ alone for your eternal salvation, let me encourage you to pray along these lines:

Dear God, I know I'm a sinner and there is nothing that I can do to save myself. I confess my complete helplessness to forgive my own sin or to work my way to heaven. At this moment I trust Christ alone as the One who took on all my sins when he died on the cross. I believe that he did everything necessary for me to live someday in your holy presence.

I thank you that Christ was raised from the dead. As best as I know how, I transfer my trust to him. I am grateful that you have promised to receive me despite my many sins and failures. Father, I take you at your word. I thank you that I can face death now that Christ is my Savior. Thank you for the assurance that you will walk with me

through death's door. Thank you for hearing my
prayer. In Jesus' name, amen.[43]

If you've prayed that prayer, take the next step and share with someone you know or perhaps someone in your family the decision you've made to follow Jesus. It will strengthen your faith and be an encouragement to someone else who may need to take that step as well.

Then make coming before the Lord in Bible Study and prayer a daily habit. Choose a time and a place, perhaps a comfy chair where you will be undisturbed, and begin to read your Bible from cover to cover.

Although it will be difficult at first—there will be many things you will not understand—prayerfully commit to sticking with it. In time, certain verses and portions of Scripture will *speak* to you personally and this will make it easier for you to share your love for Jesus with others.

Remember, too, there are many *helps* out there! Do your research online, invite others to share with you what studies they do, and pray for guidance from the Holy Spirit. The Bible tells us in John 14:26 (NIV), *"But the Advocate, the Holy Spirit, whom the Father will send in my name, will teach you all things and will remind you of everything I have said to you."* *(Emphasis, added.)*

I have been reading and studying and meditating on the Bible for over fifty years and I have learned much. But, having said that, I know there is so much more I need to learn. Studying God's Word is pleasurable for me, but my times of intercessory prayer for others is back and forth. Many of my prayers are prayer thoughts as I meditate on Scripture, rather than time spent on my knees.

Jay and I pray together before every morning, noon, and evening meal and sometimes in between. If someone calls and asks us to pray for a specific need or if the Holy Spirit prompts us to pray for a friend or loved one, we will stop what we're doing and take that need before the Lord.

For us, it's not a religious ritual but rather a habit that we both formed individually long before we met. Jay most often takes the lead in this. I join him in spirit and, when invited, verbally. We know that the Bible tells us that where two or three are gathered together, Christ is in their midst.[44]

These prayer times as a couple strengthen our relationship, and where sin needs to be confessed, it gives the repentant spouse the opportunity to do so without that feeling of being judged by the other person.

Life is short—shorter for some than for others. If you're like me, you will want to finish well. We are promised rewards for a job well done. But that's a whole other topic, isn't it?

Perhaps I'll keep that for another book.

In the meantime, I'll close this one, **Patches**, with this reminder from Paul in Philippians 3:13 (NIV): *"But one thing I do: Forgetting what is behind and straining toward what is ahead, I press on toward the goal to win the prize for which God has called me heavenward in Christ Jesus."*

About the Author

D iana Warner-Adams is a published writer whose desire it is to share the love of Jesus Christ with all who will read about her experiences in *Heaven's Scent: Spreading the Fragrance of Christ*; *Journey of Faith: Through the Looking Glass;* and her latest, *Patches.*

All three books have been published by Xulon Press within the past four years.

Diana was encouraged to study journalism many years ago by a tenth grade substitute teacher from Scotland after turning in a particular class assignment.

"You have a way with words," the teacher stated in her Scottish burr, "You should study journalism."

The seed was planted. And while Diana didn't have the financial means to attend university (nor did she even consider it!), her interest in writing blossomed over the years.

Later, several moves from east to west within the U.S. gave her opportunities to enhance her writing skills as she communicated with family and friends in both Canada and the United States.

In 1982, when returning to the Philadelphia area from Washington State, Diana joined a writer's workshop and began to write in earnest. Here she learned how to put her life's experiences on paper and submit them for publication.

Endnotes

1   After 40 years of marriage, Russ passed rather suddenly from cancer in 2002.

2   The Hebrew word for guardian-redeemer is a legal term for one who has the obligation to redeem a relative in serious difficulty (see Leviticus 25:25-55).

3   Jeremiah 29:11

4   I mention Ruth several times in Journey of Faith: Through the Looking Glass, Xulon Press, Salem Publishing, 2020.

5   Jay lived in Georgia. He had only recently returned to his hometown, Claxton, to be near his children and their growing families.

6   Name changed for privacy reasons.

7   eHarmony was the site where Jay and I got acquainted. And, yes, I was leery at first because of the stories I'd heard about dating sites, but I also relied on the discernment I felt God had given me. And, too, I wasn't about to jump into marriage with someone whose family I could not accept nor who would not accept me. I counted on my daughter Diana and her husband Dave's discernment as well. There were others I would introduce him to: my

Pastor; my friends in the community, the Church Body, and several other couples both Russ and I had grown close to over the years and who had supported me after his demise.

8   Not his real name.

9   Mark 12:29, Deut. 6:4-5, Lev. 19:18

10 Our Mum remarried two years after Dad died. It was a little hard to accept when we met Ted the first time, but I was glad Mum had found someone who was a Christian and who seemed to want to take care of her.

11 Jay (J. L.) had been widowed twice before we met. He was reaching out as he felt a man in ministry needed a partner's support. I had served the Lord through my church, both in the area of missions and evangelism, so I felt I could give him the support he needed. Serving now as his wife in interim and transitional pastoral work, I have enjoyed meeting new people (more people than whose names I can remember!) and encouraging him in his work for the Lord. He, in turn, encourages me in my writing endeavors and gives me the freedom to express myself as I feel led of the Lord to do so.

12 Jay had remarried after his wife, Jane, of 48 years had passed away with cancer. He lost his second wife, Sharon, less than five years into their marriage. Saddened but not wanting to minister alone, he reached out once again. We are both now in our senior years, but we are trusting God to keep us strong and healthy for some time yet. We love to serve in a church setting together and rely on Jesus Christ to use us to minister to those He brings across our path in varied circumstances.

13 This is all on Jay's side of the family. On my side, my grandson David and his wife, Kathleen, have given Jay

and me my first great-grandchild: Reilly Francis. Reilly was born on December 19, 2021, on his great-grand-mom's birthday on his Dad's side. His grandparents on my side are my daughter Diana and her husband, Dave.

14   Lancaster County, Pennsylvania. One of the areas in the U. S. where the Amish and Mennonite sects settled long ago and continue to live in clustered farming communities.

15   Wikipedia!

16   Philadelphia Christian Writers' Conference.

17   I go into that in more depth in Chapter 4 of my book, Heaven's Scent: Spreading the Fragrance of Christ, Xulon Press.

18   The Claxton Enterprise – November 18, 2020, p 25.

19   Names have been changed throughout.

20   Names throughout the article have been changed.

21   Tommy O'B. celebrated his 23rd birthday on 9/11/2021. A recent graduate of Kutztown University, PA, he is continuing his search for that just right position while learning and applying new skills with a local firm.

22   Etsy.

23   Psalms 1:1-3 (Journal the Word, NIV).

24   Alfred Joyce Kilmer was an American writer and poet mainly remembered for a short poem titled "Trees," which was published in the collection Trees and Other Poems in 1914. (Wikipedia)

25   Recently we drove down to the park area where we had fished that day. There is now a warning sign posted

for park users to watch out for alligators—not only in that particular pond, but in ponds, rivers and waterways throughout Florida and Georgia. Particular caution should be used, the sign noted, with small pets, as hungry alligators see them as food!

[26] Reprinted from The Conqueror/Nov.-Dec. 1987; The Christian Courier, Vol. 13 No. 12 December, 1990, (Diana Warner).

[27] See also Ezra 7:1-10 and Esther: 1:1.

[28] "This great prophecy, to be fulfilled in the millennial kingdom, is given five times in the OT: Num. 14:21; Ps. 72:19; Isa. 6:3, 11:9; and here." Ryrie Study Bible, p. 1351. Charles Caldwell Ryrie, Th.D., Ph.D.

[29] Xulon Press, 2019, p.137-139.

[30] Name changed.

[31] The VOICE of the MARTYRS, founded by Richard and Sabina Wurmbrand in 1967. To learn about VOM's statement of faith and five purposes, go to VOM. ORG/ABOUT. For ways to help the persecuted, call 800-747-0085.

[32] Vertical Take-off and Landing (VERTOL) later became a division of Boeing Defense and Space.

[33] (Dan. 2:27),

[34] Jeremiah 33:3, NIV.

[35] 1 Thessalonians 4:13-18.

[36] Philippians 4:14, The Voice Bible, Ecclesia Bible Society, Thomas Nelson.

[37] John 14:3

38   Rev. 22:12

39   Rev. 2:17

40   Rev. 3:5

41   Rev. 2:26

42   "For we know that if the earthly tent we live in is destroyed, we have a building from God, an eternal house in heaven, not built by human hands" (2 Corinthians 5:1, NIV).

43   Taken from, One Minute After You Die, Erwin W. Lutzer, www.goodnewstracts.org. or Good News Tracts, 1300 Crescent Street, Wheaton, IL 60187.

44   Matthew 18:20.

CPSIA information can be obtained
at www.ICGtesting.com
Printed in the USA
JSHW020827310123
37071JS00001B/19